W9-BPL-400

THEFT BY MORTGAGE
What "They" Don't
Want You to Know

Michael Burdick

THEFT BY MORTGAGE: What "They" Don't Want You To Know

Copyright ©2006 by Michael Burdick

This edition published by Associate Publishing Group, LLC.

ISBN 0-9787906-0-X

978-0-9787906-0-8

For my father, Lawrence D. Burdick, who taught me to stand up for myself and do the right thing rather than the easy thing.

ACKNOWLEDGEMENTS

I wish to thank Craig Jessen, Anna Salanti, and Frank Cook for their editing and support.

I also want to express my gratitude to Allan Melatti for the cover design and Candace Simpson for the cover photo.

Finally, my future wife Lakana deserves particular recognition for her patience and loving forbearance while I developed and wrote this book.

Disclaimer

In this day and age, the sad truth is that anything you say or do could likely to lead to a lawsuit. So before I begin, let me start off by saying that the wealth of information presented in this book is my own personal opinion – and only that. I am not suggesting to anyone that they have been cheated, lied to, or dealt with in a dishonest way. This book is not intended to discredit anyone in the lending or real estate industry anywhere in the world. This book has been written as an informational guide based solely on my own opinion and is for entertainment purposes only.

<u>Before you react to what you read in this book, you should check with your experts in lending, real estate, law, finance, accounting, investing, politics, religion, or even your psychic</u>.

Let me again stress that the views expressed in this book are <u>my</u> opinions. Many people in the real estate and lending industry will vehemently disagree with them. It is doubtless that they will try to discredit me by attacking me personally, and I am fine with that.

I hope that you find this book to be both informative and educational, and that you embrace the information presented as deeply as I have. But should you act on anything that you read in this book, you alone are solely responsible.

Michael Burdick

READ THIS FIRST!

Buying a home for your family is undoubtedly one of the most important financial decisions you will ever make. It is where you'll live, where you'll relax, and where you'll grow your dreams. If you are a real estate investor, you are dealing with your life savings, your retirement, and your entire financial future.

In the process, you are putting your faith in real estate professionals who may or may not be equipped to represent you properly and mortgage brokers who may or may not have your best interests at heart.

I have met REALTORs® and investors with over 20 years experience who had no idea what kind of secrets were being kept from them and how much money they had lost – until I explained it to them.

Let me ask you this: if you were to hold up a $100 bill in a room full of people and ask, *"who would like to buy this for twenty bucks?"* how many people would say *"ME!!"*?

That is correct: all of them.

Now imagine you were to ask a room full of brokers *"Who would like to pay me for giving them a loan?"* How many would raise their hands?

Right again: not one.

But they should. This book will teach you why, and give you the tools to have brokers fighting for your business. Because the truth is that brokers <u>will</u> actually pay you for your loan. Imagine that: no more origination points, garbage fees, or hidden backend profits.

This book has been laid out in a very precise order, and is intended to be read from front to back. If you want to get the most out of it, I recommend reading it straight through without skipping sections. That way I can help guide you through a wealth of information that will save you tens of thousands of dollars on all your future loans.

My first goal with this book is to help you understand your loan: where exactly your money is going, what exactly you are paying for, and who exactly is making money off your payments. I will teach you how to make mortgage brokers disclose their secret back end schemes so that you can make an INFORMED LENDING DECISION!

If you are a first time homebuyer, this book will save you from making the same mistakes that most of us have already made. It will equip you with knowledge that will allow you to buy the home of your dreams rather than settling for something less.

If you are an investor, this book will save you thousands of dollars in your transactions. It could also make you very upset to learn that you have already lost thousands because you and your agent lacked the vital information which follows.

If you are a REALTOR®, this book will save you from future liabilities and negligence. Remember: it is your sworn duty to look after your client's best interests. That includes the loan. You will never look at real estate the same after you read this, and your lenders will soon find out that their days of playing fat cat and feasting off your lack of loan knowledge are over.

If you are a mortgage broker, this book will save you nothing. In fact, you might consider relocating when your clients find out just how much money you profit from each transaction.

My second goal for this book is to empower you to write your congressman and demand stricter laws to enforce better standards of lending practices, more educational requirements for mortgage brokers, FULL DISCLOSURE of monies coming and going, and above all – **STRICT ACCOUNTABILITY**.

CONTENTS

CHAPTER 1
WHO CAN YOU TRUST?

When I became a licensed real estate agent in Florida, I thought I had found the career of my dreams. Having been blessed with the gift of the gab, I had always gravitated towards sales jobs. Having also been blessed with a strong will, I didn't want to spend my life working for someone else. So I thought real estate was the perfect path for me: it allowed me to be my own boss while spending my life talking to people. The added bonus was that it gave me the opportunity to help people during one of the most exciting times of their lives. But I didn't want to help them buy just *any* house; I wanted to help them buy the *perfect* house. And I wanted to help others sell their houses so they could move wherever their hearts desired and get there with confidence.

Imagine the satisfaction of selling a client's house for top dollar in a short amount of time and then helping them find their next house just as quickly. Now imagine getting paid for it. This is what I went to school for and studied to do. I became a REALTOR®. I took an oath to represent my clients in the strictest of standards, to protect them, and above all to be truthful in every way.

I was really starting to believe that this was the perfect career and the perfect world of business: a place where everybody had to play by the same set of rules, standards, and sense of accountability. I was wrong.

Growing up in a small town in upstate New York, going to

mass every Sunday, and serving in the Navy had helped me develop moral character. But I guess it had also left me a little naive about the financial world and completely unaware of how the real estate industry actually works. This is a world of greed, fraud, and above all, corruption. It is a world that is lacking proper education, regulation, protection, and disclosure. It is a breeding ground for lawyers, and their numbers are growing.

The more time I spent in real estate, the more I learned that it is an industry of magicians: silver tongued professionals who make our money disappear.

Imagine finding out that every time a house was bought or sold there was a 90% chance that somebody was cheated out of thousands of dollars – *and nobody ever knew it*. Except, of course, for the magician who handled the loan. And in many cases, the lender/ broker was either a friend or a family member.

How would you feel if one of your close friends or relatives made a great deal of money off of you and never told you? It happened to me. And when I found out, I was not happy. I felt conned and deceived. And when I realized how many millions of people were taken advantage of in the exact same way, I knew it was time to do something about it – even if it made a lot of people angry.

It might make you angry to learn that professionals you trusted were withholding information, and that you had to pay a great deal more than you needed to. I'm sure it's going to make many mortgage brokers angry to learn that the cat is out of the bag.

The good news is that after you read this book, no one will be able to fleece you of your money again. You will finally know just how much you are paying for your loan and to whom you can trust your business. You will be the magician with the silver tongue, and your new powers will take you straight to the bank.

CHAPTER 2
THE LOAN

First things first – before we can discuss what is wrong with the mortgage industry, we have to understand everything about it. I have put together some basic information here to ensure you understand the process and the players. In addition, there is a wealth of real estate and mortgage resources in the appendix. This book can be used as your real estate bible.

The Loan and the Uniform Residential Loan Application

"The loan" is best described as a sum of borrowed money (principal) that is generally repaid with interest. There are so many types of loans that I could write for thousands of pages and still not cover them all. So what I will do instead is go over a wide breadth of basic information and then delve into the most key pieces of information in greater detail.

When you start the loan process, the first thing you are going to encounter is the Uniform Residential Loan Application, as shown in the example on the following five pages.

Uniform Residential Loan Application

This application is designed to be completed by the applicant(s) with the Lender's assistance. Applicants should complete this form as "Borrower" or "Co-Borrower," as applicable. Co-Borrower information must also be provided (and the appropriate box checked) when ☐ the income or assets of a person other than the Borrower (including the Borrower's spouse) will be used as a basis for loan qualification or ☐ the income or assets of the Borrower's spouse or other person who has community property rights pursuant to state law will not be used as a basis for loan qualification, but his or her liabilities must be considered because the spouse or other person has community property rights pursuant to applicable law and Borrower resides in a community property state, the security property is located in a community property state, or the Borrower is relying on other property located in a community property state as a basis for repayment of the loan.

If this is an application for joint credit, Borrower and Co-Borrower each agree that we intend to apply for joint credit (sign below):

Borrower _____ Co-Borrower _____

I. TYPE OF MORTGAGE AND TERMS OF LOAN

Mortgage Applied for:	☐ VA ☐ FHA	☐ Conventional ☐ USDA/Rural Housing Service	☐ Other (explain):	Agency Case Number	Lender Case Number

Amount $	Interest Rate %	No. of Months	Amortization Type:	☐ Fixed Rate ☐ GPM	☐ Other (explain): ☐ ARM (type):

II. PROPERTY INFORMATION AND PURPOSE OF LOAN

Subject Property Address (street, city, state & ZIP):	No. of Units

Legal Description of Subject Property (attach description if necessary)	Year Built

Purpose of Loan	☐ Purchase ☐ Construction ☐ Other (explain): ☐ Refinance ☐ Construction-Permanent	Property will be: ☐ Primary Residence ☐ Secondary Residence	☐ Investment

Complete this line if construction or construction-permanent loan.

Year Lot Acquired	Original Cost $	Amount Existing Liens $	(a) Present Value of Lot $	(b) Cost of Improvements $	Total (a + b) $

Complete this line if this is a refinance loan.

Year Acquired	Original Cost $	Amount Existing Liens $	Purpose of Refinance	Describe Improvements Cost: $	☐ made ☐ to be made

Title will be held in what Name(s)	Manner in which Title will be held	Estate will be held in ☐ Fee Simple ☐ Leasehold (show expiration date)

Source of Down Payment, Settlement Charges, and/or Subordinate Financing (explain)

III. BORROWER INFORMATION

Borrower	Co-Borrower
Borrower's Name (include Jr. or Sr. if applicable)	Co-Borrower's Name (include Jr. or Sr. if applicable)

Social Security Number	Home Phone (incl. area code)	DOB (mm/dd/yyyy)	Yrs. School	Social Security Number	Home Phone (incl. area code)	DOB (mm/dd/yyyy)	Yrs. School

☐ Married ☐ Unmarried (include ☐ Separated single, divorced, widowed)	Dependents (not listed by Co-Borrower) no. ages	☐ Married ☐ Unmarried (include ☐ Separated single, divorced, widowed)	Dependents (not listed by Borrower) no. ages

Present Address (street, city, state, ZIP) ☐ Own ☐ Rent ___ No. Yrs.	Present Address (street, city, state, ZIP) ☐ Own ☐ Rent ___ No. Yrs.

Mailing Address, if different from Present Address	Mailing Address, if different from Present Address

If residing at present address for less than two years, complete the following:

Former Address (street, city, state, ZIP) ☐ Own ☐ Rent ___ No. Yrs.	Former Address (street, city, state, ZIP) ☐ Own ☐ Rent ___ No. Yrs.

IV. EMPLOYMENT INFORMATION

Borrower		Co-Borrower	
Name & Address of Employer	☐ Self Employed	Yrs. on this job	Name & Address of Employer	☐ Self Employed	Yrs. on this job
		Yrs. employed in this line of work/profession			Yrs. employed in this line of work/profession
Position/Title/Type of Business	Business Phone (incl. area code)		Position/Title/Type of Business	Business Phone (incl. area code)	

If employed in current position for less than two years or if currently employed in more than one position, complete the following:

Freddie Mac Form 65   7/05   Page 1 of 5   Fannie Mae Form 1003   7/05

	Borrower			IV. EMPLOYMENT INFORMATION (cont'd)		Co-Borrower	
Name & Address of Employer		☐ Self Employed	Dates (from – to)	Name & Address of Employer	☐ Self Employed	Dates (from – to)	
			Monthly Income $			Monthly Income $	
Position/Title/Type of Business		Business Phone (incl. area code)		Position/Title/Type of Business		Business Phone (incl. area code)	
Name & Address of Employer		☐ Self Employed	Dates (from – to)	Name & Address of Employer	☐ Self Employed	Dates (from – to)	
			Monthly Income $			Monthly Income $	
Position/Title/Type of Business		Business Phone (incl. area code)		Position/Title/Type of Business		Business Phone (incl. area code)	

V. MONTHLY INCOME AND COMBINED HOUSING EXPENSE INFORMATION

Gross Monthly Income*	Borrower	Co-Borrower	Total	Combined Monthly Housing Expense	Present	Proposed
Base Empl. Income*	$	$	$	Rent	$	
Overtime				First Mortgage (P&I)		$
Bonuses				Other Financing (P&I)		
Commissions				Hazard Insurance		
Dividends/Interest				Real Estate Taxes		
Net Rental Income				Mortgage Insurance		
Other (before completing, see the notice in "describe other income," below)				Homeowner Assn. Dues		
				Other:		
Total	$	$	$	Total	$	$

* Self Employed Borrower(s) may be required to provide additional documentation such as tax returns and financial statements.

Describe Other Income

Notice: Alimony, child support, or separate maintenance income need not be revealed if the Borrower (B) or Co-Borrower (C) does not choose to have it considered for repaying this loan.

B/C		Monthly Amount
		$

VI. ASSETS AND LIABILITIES

This Statement and any applicable supporting schedules may be completed jointly by both married and unmarried Co-Borrowers if their assets and liabilities are sufficiently joined so that the Statement can be meaningfully and fairly presented on a combined basis; otherwise, separate Statements and Schedules are required. If the Co-Borrower section was completed about a non-applicant spouse or other person, this Statement and supporting schedules must be completed about that spouse or other person also.

Completed ☐ Jointly ☐ Not Jointly

ASSETS Description	Cash or Market Value	Liabilities and Pledged Assets. List the creditor's name, address, and account number for all outstanding debts, including automobile loans, revolving charge accounts, real estate loans, alimony, child support, stock pledges, etc. Use continuation sheet, if necessary. Indicate by (*) those liabilities, which will be satisfied upon sale of real estate owned or upon refinancing of the subject property.		
Cash deposit toward purchase held by:	$			
List checking and savings accounts below		LIABILITIES	Monthly Payment & Months Left to Pay	Unpaid Balance
Name and address of Bank, S&L, or Credit Union		Name and address of Company	$ Payment/Months	$
Acct. no.	$	Acct. no.		
Name and address of Bank, S&L, or Credit Union		Name and address of Company	$ Payment/Months	$
Acct. no.	$	Acct. no.		
Name and address of Bank, S&L, or Credit Union		Name and address of Company	$ Payment/Months	$
Acct. no.	$	Acct. no.		

VI. ASSETS AND LIABILITIES (cont'd)

Name and address of Bank, S&L, or Credit Union		Name and address of Company	$ Payment/Months	$
Acct. no.	$	Acct. no.		
Stocks & Bonds (Company name/ number & description)	$	Name and address of Company	$ Payment/Months	$
		Acct. no.		
Life insurance net cash value	$	Name and address of Company	$ Payment/Months	$
Face amount: $				
Subtotal Liquid Assets	$			
Real estate owned (enter market value from schedule of real estate owned)	$			
Vested interest in retirement fund	$			
Net worth of business(es) owned (attach financial statement)	$	Acct. no.		
Automobiles owned (make and year)	$	Alimony/Child Support/Separate Maintenance Payments Owed to:	$	
Other Assets (itemize)	$	Job-Related Expense (child care, union dues, etc.)	$	
		Total Monthly Payments	$	
Total Assets a.	$	Net Worth (a minus b) ►	$	**Total Liabilities b.** $

Schedule of Real Estate Owned (If additional properties are owned, use continuation sheet.)

Property Address (enter S if sold, PS if pending sale or R if rental being held for income) ▼	Type of Property	Present Market Value	Amount of Mortgages & Liens	Gross Rental Income	Mortgage Payments	Insurance, Maintenance, Taxes & Misc.	Net Rental Income
		$	$	$	$	$	$
Totals		$	$	$	$	$	$

List any additional names under which credit has previously been received and indicate appropriate creditor name(s) and account number(s):

Alternate Name	Creditor Name	Account Number

VII. DETAILS OF TRANSACTION		VIII. DECLARATIONS				
a. Purchase price	$	If you answer "Yes" to any questions a through i, please use continuation sheet for explanation.	**Borrower**		**Co-Borrower**	
			Yes	No	Yes	No
b. Alterations, improvements, repairs		a. Are there any outstanding judgments against you?	☐	☐	☐	☐
c. Land (if acquired separately)		b. Have you been declared bankrupt within the past 7 years?	☐	☐	☐	☐
d. Refinance (incl. debts to be paid off)		c. Have you had property foreclosed upon or given title or deed in lieu thereof in the last 7 years?	☐	☐	☐	☐
e. Estimated prepaid items		d. Are you a party to a lawsuit?	☐	☐	☐	☐
f. Estimated closing costs		e. Have you directly or indirectly been obligated on any loan which resulted in foreclosure, transfer of title in lieu of foreclosure, or judgment?	☐	☐	☐	☐
g. PMI, MIP, Funding Fee		(This would include such loans as home mortgage loans, SBA loans, home improvement loans, educational loans, manufactured (mobile) home loans, any mortgage, financial obligation, bond, or loan guarantee. If "Yes," provide details, including date, name, and address of Lender, FHA or VA case number, if any, and reasons for the action.)				
h. Discount (if Borrower will pay)						
i. Total costs (add items a through h)						

Freddie Mac Form 65   7/05 Page 3 of 5 Fannie Mae Form 1003 7/05

VII. DETAILS OF TRANSACTION		VIII. DECLARATIONS					
		If you answer "Yes" to any questions a through i, please use continuation sheet for explanation.	Borrower		Co-Borrower		
			Yes	No	Yes	No	
j.	Subordinate financing						
k.	Borrower's closing costs paid by Seller	f. Are you presently delinquent or in default on any Federal debt or any other loan, mortgage, financial obligation, bond, or loan guarantee? If "Yes," give details as described in the preceding question.	☐	☐	☐	☐	
l.	Other Credits (explain)	g. Are you obligated to pay alimony, child support, or separate maintenance?	☐	☐	☐	☐	
		h. Is any part of the down payment borrowed?	☐	☐	☐	☐	
m.	Loan amount (exclude PMI, MIP, Funding Fee financed)	i. Are you a co-maker or endorser on a note?	☐	☐	☐	☐	
		---					
		j. Are you a U.S. citizen?	☐	☐	☐	☐	
n.	PMI, MIP, Funding Fee financed	k. Are you a permanent resident alien?	☐	☐	☐	☐	
		l. **Do you intend to occupy the property as your primary residence?** If "Yes," complete question m below	☐	☐	☐	☐	
o.	Loan amount (add m & n)						
		m. Have you had an ownership interest in a property in the last three years?	☐	☐	☐	☐	
p.	Cash from/to Borrower (subtract j, k, l & o from i)	(1) What type of property did you own—principal residence (PR), second home (SH), or investment property (IP)? (2) How did you hold title to the home—solely by yourself (S), jointly with your spouse (SP), or jointly with another person (O)?	____		____		

IX. ACKNOWLEDGEMENT AND AGREEMENT

Each of the undersigned specifically represents to Lender and to Lender's actual or potential agents, brokers, processors, attorneys, insurers, servicers, successors and assigns and agrees and acknowledges that: (1) the information provided in this application is true and correct as of the date set forth opposite my signature and that any intentional or negligent misrepresentation of this information contained in this application may result in civil liability, including monetary damages, to any person who may suffer any loss due to reliance upon any misrepresentation that I have made on this application, and/or in criminal penalties including, but not limited to, fine or imprisonment or both under the provisions of Title 18, United States Code, Sec. 1001, et seq.; (2) the loan requested pursuant to this application (the "Loan") will be secured by a mortgage or deed of trust on the property described in this application; (3) the property will not be used for any illegal or prohibited purpose or use; (4) all statements made in this application are made for the purpose of obtaining a residential mortgage loan; (5) the property will be occupied as indicated in this application; (6) the Lender, its servicers, successors or assigns may retain the original and/or an electronic record of this application, whether or not the Loan is approved; (7) the Lender and its agents, brokers, insurers, servicers, successors, and assigns may continuously rely on the information contained in the application, and I am obligated to amend and/or supplement the information provided in this application if any of the material facts that I have represented herein should change prior to closing of the Loan; (8) in the event that my payments on the Loan become delinquent, the Lender, its servicers, successors or assigns may, in addition to any other rights and remedies that it may have relating to such delinquency, report my name and account information to one or more consumer reporting agencies; (9) ownership of the Loan and/or administration of the Loan account may be transferred with such notice as may be required by law; (10) neither Lender nor its agents, brokers, insurers, servicers, successors or assigns has made any representation or warranty, express or implied, to me regarding the property or the condition or value of the property; and (11) my transmission of this application as an "electronic record" containing my "electronic signature," as those terms are defined in applicable federal and/or state laws (excluding audio and video recordings), or my facsimile transmission of this application containing a facsimile of my signature, shall be as effective, enforceable and valid as if a paper version of this application were delivered containing my original written signature.

Acknowledgement. Each of the undersigned hereby acknowledges that any owner of the Loan, its servicers, successors and assigns, may verify or reverify any information contained in this application or obtain any information or data relating to the Loan, for any legitimate business purpose through any source, including a source named in this application or a consumer reporting agency.

Borrower's Signature	Date	Co-Borrower's Signature	Date
X		X	

X. INFORMATION FOR GOVERNMENT MONITORING PURPOSES

The following information is requested by the Federal Government for certain types of loans related to a dwelling in order to monitor the lender's compliance with equal credit opportunity, fair housing and home mortgage disclosure laws. You are not required to furnish this information, but are encouraged to do so. The law provides that a lender may not discriminate either on the basis of this information, or on whether you choose to furnish it. If you furnish the information, please provide both ethnicity and race. For race, you may check more than one designation. If you do not furnish ethnicity, race, or sex, under Federal regulations, this lender is required to note the information on the basis of visual observation and surname if you have made this application in person. If you do not wish to furnish the information, please check the box below. (Lender must review the above material to assure that the disclosures satisfy all requirements to which the lender is subject under applicable state law for the particular type of loan applied for.)

BORROWER ☐ I do not wish to furnish this information		CO-BORROWER ☐ I do not wish to furnish this information	
Ethnicity: ☐ Hispanic or Latino ☐ Not Hispanic or Latino		Ethnicity: ☐ Hispanic or Latino ☐ Not Hispanic or Latino	
Race: ☐ American Indian or Alaska Native ☐ Asian ☐ Black or African American ☐ Native Hawaiian or Other Pacific Islander ☐ White		Race: ☐ American Indian or Alaska Native ☐ Asian ☐ Black or African American ☐ Native Hawaiian or Other Pacific Islander ☐ White	
Sex: ☐ Female ☐ Male		Sex: ☐ Female ☐ Male	
To be Completed by Interviewer This application was taken by ☐ Face-to-face interview ☐ Mail ☐ Telephone ☐ Internet	Interviewer's Name (print or type)		Name and Address of Interviewer's Employer
	Interviewer's Signature Date		
	Interviewer's Phone Number (incl. area code)		

CONTINUATION SHEET/RESIDENTIAL LOAN APPLICATION		
Use this continuation sheet if you need more space to complete the Residential Loan Application. Mark **B** for Borrower or **C** for Co-Borrower.	Borrower:	Agency Case Number:
	Co-Borrower:	Lender Case Number:

I/We fully understand that it is a Federal crime punishable by fine or imprisonment, or both, to knowingly make any false statements concerning any of the above facts as applicable under the provisions of Title 18, United States Code, Section 1001, et seq.

Borrower's Signature	Date	Co-Borrower's Signature	Date
X		X	

www.theftbymortgage.com

The Uniform Residential Loan Application exists to provide mortgage brokers the information they need to shop your credit to different servicing companies and find the best loan for your needs. There are many lending institutions from which to choose, and brokers tend to work with the ones they are best acquainted with.

In a perfect world, the broker would use the URLA to place you in the type of loan that meets all, or at least most, of your criteria. But this is not a perfect world, and most of the time brokers are just looking for the loan that will give them the biggest kickback.

What you need to realize is that lending institutions *want* your broker to bring them your application; they *want* you to pay them interest for the next 30 years. They really are *competing* for your loan. And that's why they offer huge incentives to mortgage brokers for every name that gets signed on the dotted line.

Types of Loans

Government Loans

There are only three types of government loans. They come from the FHA (Federal Housing Administration), VA (Department of Veterans Affairs) and RHS (Rural Housing Service). All others are conventional loans.

FHA Loans

The Federal Housing Administration (FHA), which is part of the U.S. Dept. of Housing and Urban Development (HUD), administers various mortgage loan programs. FHA loans usually have lower down payment requirements and are easier to qualify for than conventional loans. FHA loans cannot exceed the statutory limit.

VA Loans

VA loans are guaranteed by the U.S. Department of Veterans Affairs (VA). This guarantee allows veterans and service members to obtain home loans with more favorable terms than the public, usually with no down payment. In most cases it is easier to qualify for a VA loan than a conventional loan.

The U.S. Department of Veterans Affairs does not make loans – it guarantees loans made by lenders. The VA determines your eligibility, and if you are qualified it will issue you a certificate of eligibility to be used in applying for a VA loan.

RHS Loan Programs

The Rural Housing Service (RHS) of the U.S. Dept. of Agriculture guarantees loans for rural residents with minimal closing costs and no down payment.

Ginnie Mae, which is part of HUD, guarantees securities backed by pools of mortgage loans insured by the three federal agencies I have just discussed (FHA, VA, and RHS). Securities are sold through financial institutions that trade government securities.

Conventional Loans

Conventional loans are either *conforming* or *non-conforming*. Conforming loans have terms and conditions that follow the guidelines that have been set forth by Fannie Mae and Freddie Mac;

non-conforming loans do not.

Fannie Mae and Freddie Mac

Fannie Mae and Freddie Mac are both stockholder-owned corporations. They purchase mortgage loans complying with the guidelines from mortgage lending institutions, package the mortgages into securities, and sell the securities to investors. By doing so, Fannie Mae and Freddie Mac (like Ginnie Mae) provide a continuous flow of affordable funds for home financing that results in the availability of mortgage credit for Americans.

Fannie Mae and Freddie Mac guidelines establish the maximum loan amount, minimum to maximum borrower credit, complete income requirements, minimum down payment required, and property types. Each year these guidelines change. You may want to check to see what the current guidelines are. The 2006 conforming loan limit for a single family's first mortgage is $417,000. In 2005 it was $359,650, and in 2004 it was $333,700.

Jumbo Loans

Non-conforming loans that are above the maximum loan amount established by Fannie Mae and Freddie Mac are known as Jumbo Loans. Because Jumbo Loans are bought and sold on a much smaller scale, they often have a higher interest rate than conforming loans. But the spread between the two varies with the economy.

B, C and D Loans (Also Known as Bad Credit Loans)

Non-conforming loans that do not meet the borrower credit requirements of Fannie Mae and Freddie Mac are called

B, C & D paper loans. B, C & D paper loans are offered to borrowers who may have recently filed for bankruptcy, foreclosure, or have other derogatory marks on their credit report.

The purpose of these loans is to offer temporary financing until the borrower can qualify for conforming "A" paper financing. The interest rate in these programs tend to be much higher than "A" paper loans.

Fixed Rate Mortgages

A fixed rate mortgage (FRM) locks both the interest rate and the amount of the monthly mortgage payment for the entire period of the loan. Fixed-rate mortgages range from 10 to 40 years. The two most popular fixed rate mortgages are 15 and 30 years.

Balloon Loans

Balloon loans are short-term fixed rate loans that have fixed monthly payments based usually upon a 30-year fully amortizing schedule. A lump sum payment is due at the end of the loan's term.

The advantage of this type of loan is that the interest rate is generally lower, resulting in lower monthly payments. The disadvantage is that at the end of the term you will have to come up with a lump sum to pay off your lender.

Adjustable Rate Mortgages (ARMs)

A variable or adjustable loan is a loan whose interest rate and monthly payment fluctuates over the period of the loan. With this type of mortgage, periodic adjustments based on changes in a defined index are made to the interest rate. The index for your variable adjustable rate loan is established at the time of your loan application.

Most ARMs have an interest rate cap to protect you from huge increases in monthly payments. A lifetime cap limits the interest rate increase over the life of the loan. A periodic or adjustment cap limits how much your interest rate can rise at one time.

Negatively Amortizing Loans

I only have one thing to say about this loan: STAY AWAY!!! In my opinion, this was designed for people to get into a home that is way out of their price range by gambling that the rate of appreciation will go up faster than the rate of annual loss.

This loan puts you deeper in debt each year. If you like to gamble or have the uncanny ability to predict the future, then maybe a negatively amortizing loan is for you. But otherwise my advice is to STAY AWAY.

Option ARM Loans

This loan gives you options each month for what type of payment you'd like to make. After the first payment, you get at least three payment options to choose from each month: a minimum payment, an interest-only payment, or a 30-year amortized payment.

It takes a lot of discipline to use this loan correctly, so be careful. If you're not, you will end up like the person with the negatively amortizing loan.

The Basic Loan Process

There are nine steps in the basic loan process:

1. You meet with either a Broker or a Lender
2. You fill out a Uniform Residential Loan Application (1003 Form)
3. Your Broker or Lender runs a credit check and collects all your information
4. Your Broker or Lender submits basic information for a loan pre-approval
5. You isolate a property and submit terms needed to the Broker or Lender
6. All information is now submitted to get final loan approval
7. Loan documents are signed & closing funds are deposited
8. Loan documents are sent to the lender in exchange for loan proceeds
9. The loan is recorded

The Difference Between a Broker and a Lender

Many people think that a broker and a lender are the same thing. But they are not, and confusing the two can cost you money. Take a look at their basic definitions, and then I will delve into the differences between their duties and responsibilities.

Broker: An individual or firm who acts as an intermediary between a buyer and seller; usually charges a commission for securities and most other instruments. According to the Nevada Revised Statutes Definition (in NRS 645B.0127), a "mortgage broker" is defined as a person who, directly or indirectly:

(a) Holds himself out for hire to serve as an agent for any person in an attempt to obtain a loan which will be secured by a lien on real property;

(b) Holds himself out for hire to serve as an agent for any person who has money to lend, if the loan is or will be secured by a lien on real property;

(c) Holds himself out as being able to make loans secured by liens on real property;

(d) Holds himself out as being able to buy or sell notes secured by liens on real property; or

(e) Offers for sale in this State any security which is exempt from registration under state or federal law and purports to make investments in promissory notes secured by liens on real property.

The term does not include a person who is licensed as a mortgage banker, as defined in NRS 645E.100, unless the person is also licensed as a mortgage broker pursuant to this chapter.

Lender: The person or business making a loan that is secured by the real property of the person (mortgagor) who owes him/her/it money.

In plain English: you need a loan – you go to a mortgage broker to find you a loan – the broker goes to the lender – the lender gives the broker the money – the broker gives it to you and you pay him a fee.

Lesson #1 – Eliminate the middle man

You can bypass the middleman (the broker) and go directly to the lender or mortgagee (also known as the servicer). The broker costs you thousands of dollars, and eliminating him eliminates all the fees that would be added to your loan on his behalf.

> **HUD-1 Settlement Statement**
>
> A document that provides an itemized listing of the funds that were paid at closing.
> (See Appendix for a detailed example)

Of course I understand why people use brokers – they definitely have their advantages:

1. They have quick access to many lending institutions, which allows them to shop around quickly for the best interest rate.
2. Unlike a servicing company, mortgage brokers are required to disclose their yield spread. (Note: This does not always happen. Look closely at your HUD Settlement Statement.)

> **Yield Spread Premium (YSP)**
>
> The Bonus Paid to the Broker by the Servicer

3. Here's a third advantage your mortgage broker probably won't tell you about: you can insist that the mortgage broker pay your closing costs with the money they make on the yield spread.

Lesson #2 – Mortgage brokers are willing to pay for your business

A bank does not have to disclose their yield spread (YSP), so you will never know how much money they are really making off your deal. But using the tools provided in this book, you will be able to quickly ascertain exactly what your broker is making on his YSP. This is where your superior negotiating skills can kick in. You can use this information to your advantage and make your broker appreciate your business. Remember that his YSP can equate to tens of thousands of dollars.

When it is time to choose your next broker, think about the following things:

- Who does the broker work for? If he works for you, then one would naturally assume that his loyalty should be with you too.

- If he works for you and his loyalty is with you, then how is it that the lender is paying him so well? (Remember "A Fist Full of Dollars" with Clint Eastwood? He was paid by two different parties to do in the other. In the end, the only winner was Clint Eastwood – *The Broker*).

- Should the broker's position be further clarified?

- Should full disclosure be required in an open and easy to understand separate form?

- Should banks be required to disclose their yield spreads?

In the end, banks and brokers want your business – they want you to sign on the dotted line, and will do whatever it takes to make that happen. Every single mortgage represents tens of thousands of dollars in fees, most of which you do not know about. The banks and the brokers want your business – but they also want their industry secrets kept hidden.

Listed below are the basic requirements for doing mortgages in the state of Nevada. Requirements vary from state to state, so be sure to check your local regulations. Read them over and you will see just how scary it is: a company can hire someone and put them in the brokerage field *without any prior education or knowledge of mortgage finance.* They then have a full *two years* to complete their *ten hours* of training in order to renew. Does this sound like the kind of expertise you want representing you?

Mortgage Lending Education
NRS 645B.051 Continuing education required for renewal of license (*IT IS NOT REQUIRED FOR INITIAL APPLICATION AS A MORTGAGE AGENT*)

<u>For brokers, qualified employees and owners, directors, officers exempted from loan agent licensing requirements</u>.

By May 31 of each year, Mortgage brokers must submit to the Commissioner satisfactory proof that the each person who supervises the daily business of the mortgage broker must have completed at least 10 hours of certified courses of continuing education during the 24 months immediately preceding the date on which the license expires. Class hours used for prior renewals may not be used to meet current education requirements, although excess hours may be used or carried forward.

<u>Mortgage agents</u>. A mortgage agent who renews the license must have completed at least 10 hours of certified courses of continuing education during the 24 months immediately preceding the date on which the license expires. Class hours used for prior renewals may not be used to meet current education requirements, although excess hours may be used or carried forward.

<u>Approved course of studies</u>. The following courses of continuing education are certified to meet the continuing education requirements. To have a course approved the course will need to be approved by one of the following sponsors and relate to the mortgage industry or mortgage transactions:

1. Mortgage Bankers Association;

2. Mortgage Bankers Association of Nevada;

3. National Association of Professional Mortgage Women;

4. Nevada Association of Mortgage Professionals (successor organization to Nevada Association of Mortgage Brokers);

5. The Real Estate Division of the Department of Business and Industry; and

6. University and Community College System of Nevada.

CHAPTER 3

UNDERSTANDING YOUR HUD-1

HUD-1 Below:

A. U.S. DEPARTMENT OF HOUSING AND URBAN DEVELOPMENT SETTLEMENT STATEMENT				
B. TYPE OF LOAN			6. File Number	7. Loan Number
	1. o FHA	2. o FmHA		
3. o CONV. UNINS.	4. o VA	5. o CONV. INS.	8. Mortgage Insurance Case Number	

C. NOTE: *This form is furnished to give you a statement of actual settlement costs. Amounts paid to and by the settlement agent are shown. Items marked "(p.o.c.)" were paid outside the closing; they are shown here for informational purposes and are not included in the totals.*

D. NAME AND ADDRESS OF BORROWER:	E. NAME AND ADDRESS OF SELLER:	F. NAME AND ADDRESS OF LENDER:
G. PROPERTY LOCATION:	H. SETTLEMENT AGENT: NAME, AND ADDRESS	
	PLACE OF SETTLEMENT:	I. SETTLEMENT DATE:

J. SUMMARY OF BORROWER'S TRANSACTION	K. SUMMARY OF SELLER'S TRANSACTION

100. **GROSS AMOUNT DUE FROM BORROWER:**		400. **GROSS AMOUNT DUE TO SELLER:**	
101. Contract sales price		401. Contract sales price	
102. Personal property		402. Personal property	
103. Settlement charges to borrower(line 1400)		403.	
104.		404.	
105.		405.	
Adjustments for items paid by seller in advance		*Adjustments for items paid by seller in advance*	
106. City/town taxes to		406. City/town taxes to	
107. County taxes to		407. County taxes to	
108. Assessments to		408. Assessments to	
109.		409.	
110.		410.	
111.		411.	
112.		412.	
120. **GROSS AMOUNT DUE FROM BORROWER**		420. **GROSS AMOUNT DUE TO SELLER**	
200. **AMOUNTS PAID BY OR IN BEHALF OF BORROWER:**		500. **REDUCTIONS IN AMOUNT DUE TO SELLER:**	
201. Deposit of earnest money		501. Excess deposit (see instructions)	
202. Principal amount of new loan(s)		502. Settlement charges to seller (line 1400)	
203. Existing loan(s) taken subject to		503. Existing loan(s) taken subject to	
204.		504. Payoff of first mortgage loan	

205.		505. Payoff of second mortgage loan	
206.		506.	
207.		507.	
208.		508.	
209.		509.	
Adjustments for items unpaid by seller		*Adjustments for items unpaid by seller*	
210. City/town taxes to		510. City/town taxes to	
211. County taxes to		511. County taxes to	
212. Assessments to		512. Assessments to	
213.		513.	
214.		514.	
215.		515.	
216.		516.	
217.		517.	
218.		518.	
219.		519.	
220. **TOTAL PAID BY/FOR BORROWER**		520. **TOTAL REDUCTION AMOUNT DUE SELLER**	
300. **CASH AT SETTLEMENT FROM/TO BORROWER**		600. **CASH AT SETTLEMENT TO/FROM SELLER**	
301. Gross amount due from borrower(line 120)		601. Gross amount due to seller (line 420)	
302. Less amounts paid by/for borrower(line 220)		602. Less reductions in amount due seller (line 520)	

303. CASH (_ FROM) (_ TO) BORROWER		**603.** CASH (o TO) (o FROM) SELLER	

L. SETTLEMENT CHARGES		

700. TOTAL SALES/BROKER'S COMMISSION based on price $ @ %=	**PAID FROM**	**PAID FROM SELLER'S FUNDS AT**
Division of Commission (line 700) as follows:		
701. $ to		
702. $ to		
703. Commission paid at Settlement		
704.		
800. ITEMS PAYABLE IN CONNECTION WITH LOAN		
801. Loan Origination Fee %		
802. Loan Discount %		
803. Appraisal Fee to		
804. Credit Report to		
805. Lender's Inspection Fee		
806. Mortgage Insurance Application Fee to		
807. Assumption Fee		
808.		
809.		
810.		
811.		

900. ITEMS REQUIRED BY LENDER TO BE PAID IN ADVANCE		
901. Interest from to @$ /day		
902. Mortgage Insurance Premium for months to		
903. Hazard Insurance Premium for years to		
904. years to		
905.		
1000. RESERVES DEPOSITED WITH LENDER		
1001. Hazard Insurance months @ $ per month		
1002. Mortgage insurance months @ $ per month		
1003. City property taxes months @ $ per month		
1004. County property taxes months @ $ per month		
1005. Annual assessments months @ $ per month		
1006. Months @ $ per month		
1007. Months @ $ per month		
1008. Aggregate Adjustment months @ $ per month		
1100. TITLE CHARGES		
1101. Settlement or closing fee to		
1102. Abstract or title search to		
1103. Title examination to		
1104. Title insurance binder to		
1105. Document preparation to		

1106. Notary fees to		
1107. Attorney's fees to		
(includes above items numbers;)		
1108. Title Insurance to		
(includes above items numbers;)		
1109. Lender's coverage $		
1110. Owner's coverage $		
1111.		
1112.		
1113.		
1200. GOVERNMENT RECORDING AND TRANSFER CHARGES		
1201. Recording fees: Deed $; Mortgage $; Releases $		
1202. City/county tax/stamps: Deed $; Mortgage $		
1203. State tax/stamps: Deed $; Mortgage $		
1204.		
1205.		
1300. ADDITIONAL SETTLEMENT CHARGES		
1301. Survey to		
1302. Pest inspection to		
1303.		
1304.		

1305.		
1400. TOTAL SETTLEMENT CHARGES *(enter on lines 103, Section J and 502, Section K)*		

Source: www.hud.gov

Fees associated with the transaction but paid prior to closing are also included on the HUD. They are normally marked "POC," which means Paid Outside of Closing. These fees are an example of a lender paying a broker hidden, backend money for bringing them your loan.

When is the HUD-1 Used?

The statutes of the Real Estate Settlement Procedures Act (RESPA) require the form be used as the standard real estate settlement form in all transactions in the United States which involve federally related mortgage loans.

When is the HUD-1 Distributed?

RESPA states you should be given a copy of the HUD-1 at least one day prior to settlement. Do not assume that the HUD-1 is correct. Mistakes happen. Be sure to look things over carefully and ask questions if you do not understand something.

Section J: Summary of Borrower's Transaction

Section 100: Gross Amount Due From Borrower

Line **101** states the gross sales price of the property.

Line **102** charges for personal property (such items as draperies, washer, dryer, outdoor furniture, and decorative items being purchased from the seller).

Line **103** shows the total settlement charges to the borrower that are brought forward from Line **1400**.

Lines **104 & 105** are for amounts owed by the borrower or previously paid by the seller.

- Entries charged to the borrower include a balance in the seller's escrow account if the borrower is assuming the loan.
- The borrower may owe the seller a portion of uncollected rents.

Lines **106 - 112** are for items which the Seller has paid in advance. For instance, the buyer must reimburse the seller for his prorated portion of county taxes if the seller paid an annual bill. Each person pays charges for the time they owned the property.

Line **120** is the gross amount due from the borrower. It is the total of Lines **101** through **112**.

Section 200: Amounts Paid By or In Behalf of Borrower

These are all entries for funds the borrower will receive at closing.

Line **201** gives the buyer credit for the amount of earnest money paid when the offer was accepted.

Line **202** is the amount of the new loan, which is being paid to the borrower by the lender.

Line **203** is used when the borrower is assuming a loan or taking title subject to an existing loan or lien on the property.

Lines **204 - 209** are used to list miscellaneous items paid by or on behalf of the buyer. They may include such items as an allowance the seller is making for repairs, or replacement of items. This area is also used when the seller accepts a note from the borrower for part of the purchase price.

Lines **210 - 219** are for bills which the seller has not yet paid, but owes all or a portion of. Taxes and assessments are listed, but the area might also include rent collected in advance by the seller for a period extending beyond the settlement date.

Line **220** is the total for all items in Section 200. The total is added to the borrower's proceeds.

Section 300: Cash at Settlement From/To Borrower

Line **301** is a summary of the total amount due from the borrower.

Line **302** is a summary of all items already paid by or for the borrower.

Line **303** is the difference between lines **301** and **302**. It most often shows how much money the borrower must bring to closing. It could be a negative number, indicating that the borrower will receive funds back at closing.

Section K: Summary of Seller's Transaction

Section 400: Gross Amount Due to Seller

The amounts in this section are added to the seller's funds.

Line **401** states the gross sales price of the property.

Line **402** is for personal property (such items as draperies, washer, dryer, outdoor furniture and decorative items that the seller may be selling to the buyer).

Lines **403 - 405** are for other amounts owed by the borrower or previously paid by the seller, such as:

- If the borrower is assuming the seller's loan, he/she must reimburse the seller for the balance in the seller's escrow account.
- The buyer may owe the seller a portion of uncollected rents.

Lines **406 - 412** are for items which the Seller has paid in advance. For instance, the buyer may need to reimburse the seller for a prorated portion of county taxes if the seller paid an annual bill but will not own the property during that entire year.

Line **420** is the gross amount due to the seller. It is the total of Lines 401 through 412.

Section 500: Reductions in Amount Due to Seller

The amounts in this section are subtracted from the seller's funds.

Line **501** is used when the seller's real estate broker or another party holds the borrower's earnest money deposit, and will pay it directly to the seller.

Line **502** contains the figure from Line **1400**, the seller's total charges as computed in Section L.

Line **503** is used if the borrower is assuming or taking title subject to existing liens which are deducted from the sales price.

Lines **504 & 505** are for any first and/or second loans which will be paid-off as part of settlement (including accrued interest).

Lines **506 - 509** are shown as blank lines for miscellaneous entries.

Line **506** is used to record deposits paid by the borrower to the seller or another party who is not the settlement agent. This is slightly different than the entry in **501**. In this case the party holding the funds transfers it to the settlement agent to be disbursed at closing.

These lines may also be used to list additional liens which must be paid at settlement to clear title to the property.

Lines **510 - 519** are for bills which the seller has not yet paid, but owes all or a portion of. Taxes and assessments are listed, but the area might also include rent collected in advance by the seller for a period extending beyond the settlement date.

Line **520** is the total for all items in Section 500. The total is deducted from the seller's proceeds.

Section 600: Cash at Settlement To/From Seller

Line **601** is the gross amount due to the seller, from line 420.

Line **602** contains the total of reductions in seller's proceeds, from line **520**.

Line **603** is the difference between lines 601 and 602. It usually indicates a cash amount paid to seller, but it's possible for the seller to owe money at closing. For instance, the seller might owe more on first and second mortgages than is recovered in the contract.

Section L: Settlement Charges

This is where many entries are tabulated before being brought forward to page 1 of you HUD 1. Some columns contain charges that are paid from either the borrower's or the seller's funds. Your closing statement probably won't have entries in all the columns.

Section 700: Agency Commissions

This section deals with the commission paid to real estate agencies.

Lines **701 and 702** show how commissions are split between two participating agencies.

Commissions are usually paid from the seller's funds. However, a buyer's agent who sells a for-sale-by-owner home may be paid by his or her client, not the seller. It is important to understand that even though the agent's commission is coming from the seller's funds, the buyer is still financing that money in their loan. Many times I hear agents say that the seller is paying the commission and I strongly disagree. I say that the buyer is paying the commission and also paying to finance it over the term of the loan. The fact that it comes from the seller's settlement does not change the reality of who is being billed in the end.

Section 800: Items Payable in Connection with Loan

This is where you get blindsided by hidden points and p.o.c.'s (paid outside of closing). These items are often money that is paid to the broker for bringing your loan to the lender.

The entries on these lines are most often paid from the buyer's funds, although in some cases sellers agree to pay specified amounts to help the buyer close. This is usually done when the buyer needs closing costs to qualify for the loan. Often the costs are added to the sale price of the property and then paid by the seller at the close of escrow.

Line **801** shows the fee the lender charged for processing or originating the loan. If the fee is a percentage of the loan amount, the percentage will be stated. As an example if the loan amount was $432,000 and the fee was 1% than the broker would be paid $4,320 by the borrower at the close of escrow.

Line **802** is used to record the "points" charged by the lender. Each point is 1% of the loan amount. This is also known as buy down points in order to get the desired interest rate.

Line **803** is used to record appraisal fees. You may have paid the fee when you applied for the loan; if so, it should be marked "POC," for paid outside of closing. The amount would be shown, but would not be included in the total fees you bring to settlement.

Line **804** is used to record the cost of the credit report.

Line **805** includes charges for inspections done at the request of the lender. (note – pest and structural inspections are recorded in another area)

Line **806** is for an application fee that might be required by a Private Mortgage Insurance (PMI) company. This usually happens when the down payment is less than 20% of the loan.

Line **807** is only used for loan assumption transactions, where the buyer takes over the seller's existing mortgage. This is not done that often today.

Line **808 - 811.** are used for miscellaneous items connected with the loan. But in my opinion, these lines are more often connected to the mortgage brokers profit center, such as garbage fees paid to a mortgage broker.

Section 900: Items Required by Lender to be paid in Advance

These charges are typically paid by the buyer. They are all items which the lender requires, but which are not always paid to the lender.

Line **901** is used to record interest that is collected at settlement for the time period between closing and the first monthly payment.

Line **902** shows mortgage insurance premiums that are due at settlement. Escrow reserves for mortgage insurance are recorded later. If your mortgage insurance is a lump sum payment good for the life of the loan it should be noted.

Line **903** is used to record hazard insurance premiums that must be paid at settlement in order to have immediate insurance on the property. It is not used for insurance reserves that will go into escrow.

Lines **904** & **905** are for miscellaneous items, such as flood insurance, mortgage life insurance, credit life insurance and disability insurance premiums.

Section 1000: Reserves Deposited with Lender

This section is used to itemize escrow funds collected by the lender from the borrower for such things as hazard insurance and property taxes. The number of months charged varies, but there are limits as to how much the lender can collect.

The borrower pays current charges for the expenses in Section 900.

Lines **1001 - 1007** are for funds used to start the borrower's escrow account, from which the lender will pay next year's premiums. Each mortgage payment includes an amount that covers a portion of these recurring expenses.

Line **1008** is an escrow adjustment calculated by the settlement agent by comparing different escrow formulas. This step is to make sure the lender is not collecting more escrow funds than are allowed. The figure is always zero or a negative number.

Section 1100: Title Charges

Title charges include fees directly related to the transfer of title, such as the title examination, title search, document preparation, and fees for the title insurance policy. They are normally charged to the buyer.

Legal fees include fees for both the borrower's and seller's attorneys, and sometimes an attorney for the lender. Other items covered in this section are fees for closing agents and notaries. When one person performs many tasks, fees may be lumped together.

Line **1101** is used to record the settlement agent's fee.

Lines **1102** & **1103** are the fees for the abstract or title search and examination. If the same person performs both duties, a lump sum will be entered in line **1103**. If the person doing the work is a title company or attorney, charges are entered later, in lines **1107** or **1108**.

Line **1104** shows charges for the title insurance binder (also called a commitment to insure). Payment for title insurance policies is entered later.

Line **1105** shows charges for deed preparations, and such bills as work on mortgages and notes.

Line **1106** is the fee charged by a notary public for authenticating the execution of the settlement documents.

Line **1107** discloses an attorney's fees.

Line **1108** is the cost of title insurance (except the cost of the binder).

Lines **1109** & **1110** are informational lines that disclose the costs for the separate title insurance policies for borrower and lender. (Only line 1108 is carried forward.)

Lines **1111 - 1113** are used to enter other title-related charges which vary by location. Entries might include a fee to a county tax collector for a tax certificate or a fee to a private tax service.

Section 1200: Government Recording and Transfer Charges

This section is used to itemize charges such as costs for recording deeds and mortgages and fees for tax stamps.

Sections 1300 & 1400: Additional Settlement Charges and Totals

Section **1300** is used to record survey fees and inspections for such things as pests, lead-based paint, and radon. Structural inspections and inspections for heating, plumbing, or electrical equipment might also be included. If either party is buying a home warranty, the charge will be entered in this section.

Line **1400** is for the total settlement charges paid from borrower's and seller's funds. They are also entered in Sections J and K, lines **103** and **502**.

CHAPTER 4
YOUR REALTOR®

Let me begin by saying that I am a REALTOR® and proud of it. I truly believe that I have a purpose in the world of real estate to help my clients in their quest to own a home; a goal which has become an integral part of the American dream. REALTORs® subscribe to a strict code of ethics and are required to have ongoing education in their field in order to maintain their licenses. REALTORs® are aware that consumers are not required to use their services. That is why they can truly classify themselves as being employed by you, the client.

What Is a REALTOR®?
Reprinted from The Greater Las Vegas Association of REALTORs® Web Site (www.glvar.net)

A real estate agent is a REALTOR® when they become a member of the NATIONAL ASSOCIATION OF REALTORS®, The Voice for Real Estate® — the world's largest professional association. The term REALTOR® is a registered collective membership mark that identifies a real estate professional who is a member of the NATIONAL ASSOCIATION OF REALTORS® and subscribes to its strict Code of Ethics.

Founded in 1908, NAR has grown from its original nucleus of 120 to over 800,000 members today. NAR is composed of REALTORS® who are involved in residential and commercial real estate as brokers, salespeople, property managers, appraisers, counselors and others engaged in all aspects of the real estate industry.

Members belong to one or more of some 1,700 local associations/boards and 54 state and territory associations of REALTORS®. They can join one of our many institutes, societies and councils. Additionally, NAR offers members the opportunity to be active in our appraisal and international real estate specialty sections. REALTORS® are pledged to a strict Code of Ethics and Standards of Practice. Working for America's property owners, the NATIONAL ASSOCIATION OF REALTORS® provides a facility for professional development, research and exchange of information among its members.

REASONS TO USE A REALTOR®
(from the Nevada State Realty Board)

You may be thinking about selling your home yourself and not contracting with a REALTOR®. Here are some things to consider about the value a professional real estate agent provides to you when selling your home.

REALTORs® can provide an objective look at your home and make suggestions to make your home more marketable.

As professionals, REALTORs® understand the market and the special considerations of your neighborhood. They know what will sell and what buyers are looking for.

REALTORs® have an understanding of the current market conditions and values.

This may lead to a quicker sale and possibly top dollar.

They will know how to price your home so that it will sell in a reasonable amount of time and you will get the most value from that sale as possible. The longer a home is in on the market due to lack of exposure, the more likely a prospective buyers assumes there is a problem with the home.

REALTORs® can get more exposure for your home.

The Multiple Listing Service is a database of homes for sale that most REALTORs® have access to. It is the fastest and easiest way to get your home in front of thousands of REALTORs® instantly. Additionally, most REALTORs® now have web sites to provide even greater exposure for you home to potential buyers.

REALTORs® will write your ads and place them in the newspaper or in a professional real estate magazine.

REALTORs® are not only real estate experts, but they also understand the methods of successfully marketing your home to get the interest of buyers. They have the resources and mechanisms to get your home in front of thousands of buyers.

Agents provide quality and eye catching street signs to insure high visibility, along with flyers containing details of your home.

A professional looking and attractive sign in front of the home with easy to access details sets the expectation to the buyer that they are dealing with professionals. It gives everyone confidence in moving forward in the sales process.

You will have the confidence and security of not dealing with strangers in your home.

REALTORs® know how to pre-screen potential buyers to know who is serious and who is not. They will not let "just anyone" walk through your home.

You do not need to be present to show your home.

Professional REALTORs® work with buyers by appointment and brings them to see your home. You can continue your daily routines and weekend activities without having the disruption of waiting for potential buyers who never come when they say they will or do not show up at all.

REALTORs® can provide an electronic lockbox so other REALTORs® may show your property.

This is a secure device that safely stores your house key so other REALTORs® can bring buyers to see your home. This makes it more convenient for other real estate professionals and their buyers to view your home.

REALTORs® can conduct informative and professional tours of your home through open houses.

REALTORs® will commit their time and staff to advertising and hosting an open house to show your home to many buyers. This is a way of capturing buyers who are just looking and a great way for the REALTOR® to qualify their intentions before you need to deal with them.

REALTORs® who provide the buyer will get the buyer

pre-qualified.

Successful REALTORs® work with buyers whom they know qualify for the financial requirements to purchase your home. They usually have a relationship with a mortgage lender and work together to qualify buyers.

There is less chance of missing details when negotiating the offer.

REALTORs® are professionally trained and have the support of a broker, so they know all the legal points and negotiating points to address when negotiating on your behalf.

There are fewer emotions involved with questions regarding the property and its sale.

Selling your home can be an emotional experience. The REALTOR®, acting on your behalf, can insulate you from potentially uncomfortable situations in the negotiating process.

The seller is required by law to provide disclosures in writing on lead based paint, mold and pest issues.

The seller must supply a Real Property Disclosure form that details the condition of the property. The seller must also provide a Home Owners Association package that includes CC&Rs, by-laws, minutes, budgets and any lawsuits. In addition, the seller must disclose any information on highways, casinos and landfills (contamination) that will affect the property. The REALTOR® would be responsible for all the above disclosures.

REALTORs® usually have a relationship with the lenders and escrow officers, which can expedite the process.

Because they transact real estate sales on a monthly basis, REALTORs® have strong business relationships with the other companies and individuals who need to be involved in making sure the sale gets completed properly and efficiently.

A real estate agent can assist in helping you find a new home.

Once you have established a good working relationship with your REALTOR®, you now have a strong ally to work on your behalf finding a new home for you and your family.

CHAPTER 5
ESCROW & TITLE

What is Escrow?

The following is a description of what an escrow is and the role the title company plays in the real estate transaction. There are also directions on how to open an escrow and a sample and explanation of escrow instructions.

The title company is a disinterested third party who collects and disburses funds in a real estate transaction in accordance with the written agreement for the sale (Offer & Acceptance) between a buyer and a seller. The title company receives the Offer & Acceptance signed by the seller and buyer. The earnest money from the buyer is also received at that time and escrow is then officially opened. The earnest money is deposited and an escrow number is assigned to the file.

Earnest Money
The check that accompanies the Offer to Buy

From this point forward, any monies, documents, and/ or deeds are disbursed in accordance with the written agreement. The escrow officer's primary responsibility is to comply with written instructions that have been agreed to by all parties in the transaction. A real estate agent or broker represents the principals to the transaction, and it is inappropriate for the escrow officer to act on verbal instructions.

The title company will issue "Escrow Instructions" stating its exact responsibilities in completing the sales transaction. It will identify all parties in the transaction and the terms under which all monies and documents will be disbursed.

The title company will also perform a "Title Search." This process involves identifying any parties who have an interest in the property, as well as other considerations such as identifying any easements. At the closing, they will issue a "Title Insurance Policy." The policy will insure the buyer against any undisclosed recorded items affecting the property. A fee is charged for the policy. Title Insurance is a prudent measure taken to protect the buyer and their lender.

Once escrow is opened, the escrow officer will prepare the necessary documents and forward copies of the Escrow Instructions and Addendum to the parties, including the agents representing the buyer and seller. An initial review of the instructions will insure that the names are correct, that the right property is being sold, and that all the terms of the original contract are included.

After the Escrow Instructions, an appointment with the escrow officer is appropriate to sign the escrow documents. It is best to have escrow papers signed immediately as it memorializes the escrow officer's duties. Escrow is not officially open until all parties have signed the Escrow Instructions.

During the escrow period, the escrow officer will provide copies of the Preliminary Title Report and all Demands and Beneficiary Statements for review. Again, an immediate review may offset future issues.

When closing is near, call the escrow officer for an appointment. You will need to discuss the file to insure all the required items have been handled.

Advise your Escrow Officer of the scheduled closing date early enough to allow time for final calculations, such as updating any loan payoff. The Title Company will read the loan documents to make the calculations, and the lenders costs are needed to finalize the buyer's deposit and funds. Escrow can provide an estimated worksheet with the information they have, however it will not be exact and could inconvenience the parties. The Escrow Officer will provide the agents a copy of the worksheet or estimated closing statement for their review.

Funds SHOULD BE IN THE FORM OF CASH, CASHIER'S CHECK OR DIRECT WIRE INTO THE ESCROW TRUST ACCOUNT. A personal check may delay the closing until the check can be cleared.

The next page shows a flow chart breaking down the basic escrow process from start to finish.

ESCROW & TITLE FLOW CHART

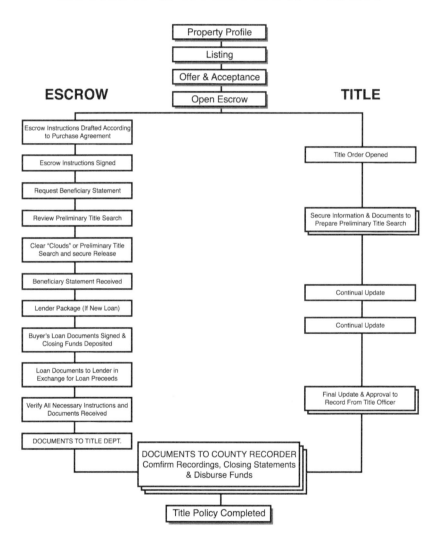

Escrow Checklist

- Are all the documents signed?
- Has the Buyer obtained their fire insurance?
- Have all the contingencies been satisfied?
- If required, has the termite inspection been completed?
- If it is a new loan, has the Buyer been approved?
- Has the Home Warranty been ordered?

How to Open Escrow

It is always advisable to set up an appointment with the Escrow Officer to meet in person to go over the transaction together.

Items Needed to Open Escrow

- Clear copy of the fully completed and signed Offer and Acceptance.
- Copies of ALL counter offers and/or addenda. (Note: If you have more than one counter offer, please number them at the top of the page.)
- Provide the name, address, and correct loan numbers on all existing loans. A copy of the seller's payment coupon is the best way to insure the accuracy of the information.
- Provide the name, address, and phone number of any cooperating Real Estate Agent. A business card is most helpful. Also remember to provide the amount of commission and the split.
- Provide the name, address, and phone number of the Loan Officer on any new loan. Again, a business card is best.
- Buyers and Sellers full names, phone numbers, and

current mailing address.
- Submit a completed Statement of Information, a copy of the Sellers Deed, Title Policy, or a copy of the Property Profile you may have obtained.
- A completed Opening Checklist

Escrow Instructions

Here is a brief explanation of items found in Escrow Instructions. Be aware that all title companies' Escrow Instructions are not alike.

Escrow Number

This is the identifying number of your Escrow. The initials at the end of each number identify the Escrow Officer handling the transaction. If you have this information, it saves time when locating your file.

Branch Address

The location of the office handling your escrow.

Consideration Instructions

Shows the earnest money, financing terms, down payment, and sales price of the contract.

Seller

Full names of sellers — check for spelling to insure the names are correct.

Buyer

Full names of buyers — check for spelling to insure the names are correct.

Legal Description

The full legal description will appear here, unless it is metes and bounds. Be sure the property description is correct.

Street Address

Check for accuracy and do not forget to include the correct city and zip code.

APN

The APN is the Tax Assessors Parcel Number. Check this against your information.

Title Insurance

The buyers and new lender require that they be provided with a Policy of Title Insurance, we will indicate what kind of policy is to be issued.
1.   Cash or assumptions no new loans....Owners
2.   Assumptions with note to seller....Joint Protection
3.   New financing....Owners and ALTA

Buyer

Buyers are listed again and how they have chosen to take title. If the O&A vesting is not addressed we will have Buyers execute a separate instruction.

Subject to

This area shows items of record that will be on the title policy as exceptions:
1. Current taxes…. always a lien (not always due)
2. CC & R's

Terms and Conditions

This area is where all the terms and conditions of the sale are found.
1. Loans to be assumed
2. Contingencies
3. New loans
4. Other requirements
5. Any item not handled by the Escrow Officer will be shown on an addendum such as; personal property, possession, seller warranties, etc.

Signature Page

Sets out that both buyer and seller have read and agreed to the escrow instructions, and addresses estimated costs per their agreement.

What is Title Insurance?

It is protection against loss if a covered defect is found in your title. When you buy a home, you are given a title to the property, which generally means you receive full legal ownership. Sometimes, however, there may be a hidden mistake in a prior deed, will, mortgage etc. that may give someone else a valid legal claim against your property.

Why is Title Insurance Important?

It provides a "safety fence" around your property. When you buy property, you are commonly required to buy title insurance. This covers the outstanding balance on the mortgage for the lender, but does not protect you. When acquiring property, it is a good idea to get your own title insurance policy. It will give you maximum protection in case there is a claim against your home

How Can There Be A Title Defect if the title has been searched and a loan policy issued?

Title insurance is issued after a careful examination of the public records. But even the most thorough search cannot absolutely assure that no title hazards are present. In addition to matters shown by public records, other title problems may exist that cannot be disclosed in a search.

Against what does title insurance protect?

Here are some common hidden risks that can cause loss of title or create an encumbrance on title:

- False impersonation of the true owner of the property
- Forged deeds, releases or wills
- Undisclosed or missing heirs
- Instruments executed under invalid or expired power of attorney
- Mistakes in recording legal documents
- Misinterpretations of wills
- Deeds by persons of unsound mind
- Deeds by minors
- Deeds by persons supposedly single, but in fact

married
- Liens for unpaid estate, inheritance, income or gift taxes
- Fraud

What protection does title insurance provide against defects and hidden risks?

Title insurance will pay for defending against any lawsuit attacking the title of the insured, and will either clear up title problems or pay the insured's losses. An insured is an owner, lender or a party having and interest in Real property. For a one-time premium, a title insurance policy remains in effect as long as the insured, or the insured's successors or assigns, retain an interest in the property, or have any obligations under a warranty in any conveyance of it. Owner's title insurance, issued simultaneously insuring the lender through a loan policy, is the best title insurance value a property owner can get.

Source: Nevada Title Company Website
www.nevadatitle.com/

CHAPTER 6
WHAT IS WRONG WITH TODAY'S LOAN?

I have always subscribed to the age-old KISS philosophy, also known as ***"keep it simple, stupid."***

The biggest problem in the mortgage industry? Nothing is simple. Things are drawn out for no apparent reason other than to keep the consumer confused. This is the first problem with today's loans: they are too difficult to figure out.

The language of mortgage agreements is so thick that it would take a genius to figure out what the heck is being said. The reason, of course, is that if you were to distill what they are saying, a very simple phrase would emerge: prepare to be hurt financially.

Most contracts include the Latin words *caveat emptor*. Let the buyer beware.

Think about it – why is it hidden in Latin? Why not just come out and say "let the buyer beware?" How many people in America speak Latin today? Perhaps we should take our loans to a catholic priest and have him decipher them for us. Perhaps this is a round about way of saying we should pray to God if we are about to take out a mortgage loan.

The point I am making is this:

<u>Loans should be simple and easy to read.</u>

Loans should state:

- The amount being borrowed
- The set interest rate
- The length of the loan
- The total payouts, both short and long term
- All fees and all parties being paid
- The lender and lendee information
- The terms agreed to

But instead, loan documents are complicated to the point of absurdity. And because most people are so busy trying to qualify for a loan and a specific interest rate, they completely overlook what the loan obligates them to do. Key issues such as prepayment penalties, late fees, amortization rate changes, and huge fees all slide under their radar. And missing those items can make an enormous difference on the true cost of your loan.

The second problem with today's loans is that loan agreements do not disclose all the facts, and end up being unfavorable to the borrower. There are two reasons that I say this:

1) They do not disclose where all your money is actually going.

2) They do not show you how your loan was shopped.

I'm going to explain to you how the loan process works from the broker's point of view. Once you can see things from their side of the table, you'll have a much better ability to bargain. This could save you thousands of dollars.

First, I want to deal with the "origination fee." Or as I like to call it, the biggest scam in the history of lending. To put it simply, the origination fee is what the mortgage broker charges you for finding a lender. What they will not tell you, and what they do not want you to know, is that the very same lender is *also* paying them *for the exact same service.*

Isn't that being paid twice for the same job?

Take a look at the example:

L. Settlement Charges							Paid From Borrowers Funds at Settlement	Paid From Seller's Funds at Settlement
700. Total Sales/Broker's Commission based on price $244,900.00			@	6% =	$14,694.00			
Division of Commission (line 700) as follows:								
701.	$7,347.00	to	Listing Agent					
702.	$7,347.00	to	Buyers Agent					
703. Commission paid at Settlement								$14,694.00
704.								
800. Items Payable In Connection With Loan								
801. Loan Origination Fee	1 %						$ 2449.00	
802. Loan Discount	%							
803. Appraisal Fee	to							
804. Credit Report	to	Mortgage Company					$12.39	
805. Lender's Inspection Fee							$650.00	
806. Mortgage Insurance Application Fee to								
807. Assumption Fee								
808. Processing Fee To: Mortgage Company							$995.00	
809. Administration Fee To: Mortgage Company							$2,204.00	
810. Premium Paid By Lender To: Mortgage Company			$6,612.00					
811. Tax To : Lender							$70.00	
900. Items Required By Lender To Be Paid In Advance								
901. Interest from	to	@ $	/day					
902. Mortgage Insurance Premium for			months to					
903. Hazard Insurance Premium for			years to					
904.			years to					
905.								

After the broker double bills his service, he then increases the interest rate of the loan at the front end to create profit points for himself when the loan closes. Let me explain.

If you are approved by the lender at an interest rate of 6.50% and the broker has you sign for a loan with 7% interest, then he is making a profit of 0.5%, which will be paid out to him at closing.

What this adds up to is easily calculated by taking the loan amount and multiplying it by 0.005.

EXAMPLE:

$359,000 Loan Amount

X .005 0.5 Percent

= $1,795 Profit to the Broker

That $1,795 is money that is coming from *your* monthly payments.

What is significant about this is that your broker is profiting from you without your knowledge. This form of money making is called hedging points, increasing their yield spread, or increasing their profit margin. It is easily hidden and hard to detect. Many brokers will not do a loan unless there is a minimum profit margin involved. When brokering a relatively small loan, this technique is commonly used to increase their bottom line.

Another way to cheat you out of your hard earned money is by creating what are called "garbage fees," as circled in the example below.

L. Settlement Charges						Paid From Borrowers Funds at Settlement	Paid From Seller's Funds at Settlement
700. Total Sales/Broker's Commission based on price $244,900.00		@	6% =	$14,694.00			
Division of Commission (line 700) as follows:							
701.	$7,347.00	to	Listing Agent				
702.	$7,347.00	to	Buyers Agent				
703. Commission paid at Settlement							
704.							$14,694.00
800. Items Payable In Connection With Loan							
801. Loan Origination Fee		%					
802. Loan Discount		%					
803. Appraisal Fee		to					
804. Credit Report		to	Mortgage Company			$12.39	
805. Lender's Inspection Fee						$650.00	
806. Mortgage Insurance Application Fee to							
807. Assumption Fee							
808. Processing Fee To: Mortgage Company						$995.00	
809. Administration Fee To: Mortgage Company						$2,204.00	
810. Premium Paid By Lender To: Mortgage Company			$6,612.00				
811. Tax To : Lender						$70.00	
900. Items Required By Lender To Be Paid In Advance							
901. Interest from	to	@ $		/day			
902. Mortgage Insurance Premium for				months to			
903. Hazard Insurance Premium for				years to			
904.				years to			
905.							

These fees are created simply to increase the broker's overall profit margin. They would have you believe you are paying for legitimate loan-related expenses, but in actuality they are making you underwrite their day-to-day operational costs. Through bogus administration fees and fake evaluations, they have you paying for every paperclip, every staple, and every drop of air-conditioning they use. Call me crazy, but I believe their everyday costs of doing business should not be passed on to you, the consumer.

Then, of course, there is the prepayment penalty, of which there are two types. The first is a hard prepayment penalty, which means that if you sell or refinance your loan during a specific period of time (usually one to three years), you will be charged a very large fee – often the equivalent of six months to one year of payments. The second is called a soft prepayment penalty, which charges you a penalty for refinancing, but not selling. This latter type is not common.

How do lenders get you to sign a prepayment penalty? Their man on the inside, of course: the broker. If the broker gets you to sign a prepayment penalty, they are rewarded with a percentage of the total loan cost (usually 2%) when the loan is closed. That adds up to big bucks for the broker, as seen in the example below:

$359,000 (Loan Amount)
X .02 (2 percent)
=$7180 Profit to the Broker

The reason lenders want a prepayment penalty is to insure that they will make at least one to three years of interest off your money. One of the reasons they are so eager to have that insurance is to keep them from losing the large amount of money they paid the broker to get your business in the first place.

This small piece of information could save you tens of thousands of dollars, and will be discussed in greater detail in later chapters.

So never forget for a second that loans are written on behalf of the lender, and that brokers are not going to make as big of a profit if they puts your best interests first.

People get confused about this because their professional real estate relationships are built on trust and faith, and they are used to seeing very open documents. When you purchase a home using a REALTOR®, your agent uses a *buyers contract*, which is designed to protect you. When you sell your home using a REALTOR®, your agent uses a *listing agreement*, which is also designed to protect you. When both the buyer and the seller have REALTORs®, they use these contracts in conjunction with an additional form called a *counter*. The purpose of using multiple forms is to provide equal protection for both sides of the transaction, and to represent both in a fair and honest way.

But with mortgage loans this is not the case. Instead there is only one form, and it's designed to protect the lender and make the broker rich. It provides you with no protection whatsoever. Worse, it uses Latin phrases, difficult calculations, huge drawn out fractions, and enough verbiage to put an accountant to sleep – all in an effort to keep you in the dark.

SO ONCE AGAIN - WHAT IS WRONG WITH TODAY'S LOANS?

1. They are not simple, they are not easy to understand.

2. They are too long.

3. They are mathematically challenging for most people.

4. They are favorable to only one party: the lender.

5. They are dishonest.

6. They lack protection for the consumer.

7. They conceal too much valuable information from the consumer.

8. There are too many types out there to know what is best.

9. There is no accountability on the part of the broker.

10. There is a huge lack of legislation.

11. There is a huge amount of fraud.

CHAPTER 7
THE SECRET CONSPIRACY

Conspiracy:
1. <u>An agreement to perform together an illegal, wrongful, or subversive act.</u>
2. <u>An agreement between two or more persons to commit a crime or accomplish a legal purpose through illegal action.</u>
3. <u>A secret agreement between two or more people to perform an unlawful act.</u>

What you have to fully comprehend is that this is not the story of a crooked broker in a back alley office. This is not about hucksters who fly into town, steal everyone's money, and then disappear. This is the story of the brokers, the bankers, and even your elected officials. Everyone is making money here except you. American consumers are having their bones picked clean and then left in the desert to rot.

The mortgage brokers and loan officers work together for the completely legitimate purpose of shopping your loan for you, but are disloyal to you in their efforts. Through evasion and a lack of full disclosure, they are ensuring that you do not have the proper knowledge to best negotiate your loan. There are numerous cases right now showing fraud and predatory lending issues with brokerages worldwide, but these are the same people who are making illegal campaign contributions to government officials in order to continue doing what they do. They're paying off your elected officials to keep them from protecting you and your money.

Even when these sharks get caught they manage to chew their way out of the net. They plea bargain, pay money to the system (which is a pittance compared to what they steal), and are back on the street without so much as an apology or even the slightest admittance of wrongdoing. If you or I were caught stealing candy from the store, we would be dragged into court and held up as a criminal for all to see. But if you're a multi-billion dollar corporation, you can wipe your nose with people's financial future and never even have to say you're sorry.

For example, on January 23, 2006, the State of New Hampshire announced that Ameriquest Mortgage had agreed to pay a 325 million dollar settlement in a class action lawsuit filed from 49 states. But even though the settlement was the second largest state or federal consumer protection settlement in recorded history, and even though part of the plea involved a pledge to change their business practices, *Ameriquest never admitted to any wrongdoing.*

The largest case of direct restitution was paid out in 2002 by Household Finance. They had unfairly overcharged borrowers to the point where many had lost their homes. The settlement figure was 484 million dollars. While many politicians lauded the settlement as being a watershed event that would forever change the face of the American mortgage business, the more pragmatic Association of Community Organizations for Reform Now (ACORN) pointed out that not only was the figure pathetic compared to what they had stolen, the restitution was "puny" compared to what the victims had suffered. And to add insult to injury, the closest that chairman and CEO William Aldinger came to expressing contrition was stating: "We apologize to our customers *for not always living up to their expectations.*"

But how can they get away with it? How can they fleece billions, and then get off with a plea of millions? Because they have members of congress in their pocket. A recent and tragically insidious example is the "Responsibility and Lending Act" proposed on the House floor by Robert Ney, a Republican representative from Ohio. Disguised as a bill to fight predatory spending, in reality the bill does the opposite. By superseding existing state laws (many of which have very harsh restrictions for lenders and very broad protections for consumers), the bill would set back the work against predatory lending across the entire country with a single blow.

Fortunately the system's corruption, while rampant, is not complete. Democratic representatives Mel Watt, Brad Miller, and Barney Frank (the first two from North Carolina, the latter from Massachusetts) have proposed a counter bill called the "Prohibit Predatory Lending Act." This bill, which is supported by consumer advocacy groups such as the Center for Responsible Lending, is modeled after North Carolina state laws, which are generally considered the strictest laws against predatory lending in the nation.

Which bill will pass? We'll have to wait and see. But the mortgage industry is already showering Ney with money – including a ten thousand dollar contribution from the Mortgage Bankers Association and another ten grand from the National Association of REALTORs®.

The conspiracy exists, and so long as it's allowed to perpetuate itself, you the consumer will continue to pay – literally.

CHAPTER 8
OPERATION QUICK FLIP

If you still need proof of a conspiracy, go to the Federal Bureau of Investigation's web site (www.fbi.gov). You will find headline archives of multiple types of fraud and corruption throughout the lending industry. There is so much illegal activity that the FBI has assigned a task force to manage the deluge of cases.

You will be shocked to learn that in the 2004 fiscal year consumers were cheated out of $429,000,000. In the 2005 fiscal year, that number more than doubled to a staggering $1,014,000,000. That's over one billion dollars in reported losses to mortgage consumers just like you.

And of course the money doesn't just go to the brokers and the lenders. It's shared with the lobbyists and the politicians. Our government's halls are lined with money that bought the votes to keep the lending laws in favor of the lenders. With over one billion dollars to spread around, it's no wonder that the mortgage industry feels safe. Congress cannot afford to stop it.

OPERATION QUICK FLIP

Operation Quick Flip is designed to show that federal law enforcement recognizes the mortgage fraud threat. The Federal Bureau of Investigation Criminal Investigative Division (CID), the Department of Housing and Urban Development (HUD) Office of the Inspector General

(OIG), the United States Postal Inspection Service (USPS), the Internal Revenue Service (IRS), and the Department of Justice (DOJ) have participated in this case round-up to provide information to the public regarding the federal government's efforts to combat mortgage fraud. The federal agencies involved are targeting mortgage fraud groups in order to disrupt and dismantle them permanently.

Mortgage Fraud is one of the fastest growing white collar crimes in the United States. Mortgage Fraud is defined as a material misstatement, misrepresentation, or omission relied upon by an underwriter or lender to fund, purchase, or insure a loan.

There are two types of Mortgage Fraud: fraud for property and fraud for profit. Fraud for Property, also known as Fraud for Housing, usually involves the borrower as the perpetrator on a single loan. The borrower makes a few misrepresentations, usually regarding income, personal debt, and property value or there are down payment problems. The borrower wants the property and intends to repay the loan. Sometimes industry professionals are involved in coaching the borrower so that they qualify. Fraud for Property/Housing accounts for 20 percent of all fraud.

Fraud for profit involves industry professionals. There are generally multiple loan transactions with several financial institutions involved. These frauds include numerous gross misrepresentations including: income is overstated, assets are overstated, collateral is overstated, the length of employment is overstated or fictitious employment is reported, and employment is backstopped by co-conspirators. The borrower's debts are not fully disclosed, nor is the borrower's credit history, which is often altered. Often, the borrower assumes the identity of another person (straw buyer). The borrower states he intends to use the property for occupancy when he/she intends to use the property for rental income, or is purchasing the property for another party (nominee). Appraisals almost always list the property as owner-occupied. Down payments do not exist or are borrowed and disguised with a fraudulent gift letter. The property value is inflated (faulty appraisal) to increase the sales value to make up for no down payment and to generate cash proceeds in fraud for profit.

Typical fraud schemes:

Backward Applications: After identifying a property to purchase, a borrower customizes his/her income to meet the loan criteria.

Air Loans: These are non-existent property loans where there is usually no collateral. An example would be where a broker invents borrowers and properties, establishes accounts for payments and maintains custodial accounts for escrows. They may set up an office with a bank of telephones, each one used as the employer, appraiser, credit agency, etc. for verification purposes.

Silent Seconds: The buyer of a property borrows the down payment from the seller through the issuance of a non-disclosed second mortgage. The primary lender believes the borrower has invested his own money in the down payment, when in fact, it is borrowed. The second mortgage may not be recorded to further conceal its status from the primary lender.

Nominee Loans: The identity of the borrower is concealed through the use of a nominee who allows the borrower to use the nominee's name and credit history to apply for a loan.

Property Flips: Property is purchased, falsely appraised at a higher value, and then quickly sold. What makes property flipping illegal is that the appraisal information is fraudulent. The schemes typically involve fraudulent appraisals, doctored loan documents, and inflation of the buyer's income.

Foreclosure schemes: The subject identifies homeowners who are at risk of defaulting on loans or whose houses are already in foreclosure. Subjects mislead the homeowners into believing that they can save their homes in exchange for a transfer of the deed and up-front fees. The subject profits from these schemes by re-mortgaging the property or pocketing the fees paid by the homeowner.

Equity Skimming: An investor may use a straw buyer, false income documents, and false credit reports to obtain a mortgage loan in the straw buyer's name. Subsequent to closing, the straw buyer signs the property over to the investor in a quit claim deed which relinquishes all rights to the property and provides no guaranty to title. The investor does not make any mortgage payments and rents the property until foreclosure takes place several months later.

Federal law enforcement is working with state and local law enforcement, regulators, and the financial institution industry to combat the problem.

OFHEO (Office of Federal Housing Enterprise Oversight)

has passed a regulation requiring Freddie Mac and Fannie Mae to report suspicious mortgage fraud activity on a Mortgage Incident Notice (MFIN).

FBI, OFHEO, and FinCEN (Financial Crimes Enforcement Network) are working to establish a reporting device similar to the banking industry's Suspicious Activity Report. This is in progress, but will likely take some time as regulations and possibly legislation will have to be passed.

The FBI, HUD-OIG, USPS, and IRS conduct criminal investigations into Mortgage Fraud Activity with a goal of disrupting and dismantling mortgage fraud rings. We strongly support joint investigations to effectively utilize all of our limited resources while strengthening investigations by tapping into everyone's expertise.

From July 5, 2005, until October 27, 2005, the FBI, HUD-OIG, USPS, IRS, in coordination with the DOJ, indicted 156 mortgage fraud subjects. A total of 81 arrests were made. A total of 89 convictions were obtained, and 60 subjects were sentenced during this time frame.

The combined loss to the industry by the above-subjects is $606,830,604.

In fiscal year 2005, the following stats are available:

- 21,994 SARs were filed (up from 17,127 in Fiscal Year 2004).

- 721 pending FBI Mortgage Fraud cases (up from 534 in Fiscal Year 2004).

- 1,020 pending HUD-OIG Mortgage Fraud cases (up from 920 in Fiscal Year 2004).

- 206 FBI indictments/informations (down from 241 in Fiscal Year 2004).

- 170 FBI convictions (consistent with 172 convictions in Fiscal Year 2004)

- $1,014,000,000 (FBI) reported loss (up from $429,000,000 in Fiscal Year 2004).

Top ten hot spots for Mortgage Fraud activity in 2003 (per capita): California, Nevada, Utah, Colorado, Missouri, Illinois, Michigan, South Carolina, Georgia, and Florida.

Top ten hot spots for Mortgage Fraud activity in 2004 (per capita): California, Nevada, Utah, Arizona, Colorado, Missouri, Illinois, Maryland, Georgia, and Florida.

CASES:

OPERATION BROKEN LOAN (Detroit): On 10/18/2005, an undercover operation targeting five criminal mortgage fraud organizations culminated in the execution of 18 arrest warrants, seven search warrants, eight seizure warrants for subjects' bank accounts, and two vehicle seizures. Among those charged were several mortgage brokers in the Detroit metropolitan area who allegedly defrauded mortgage lenders through inflated appraisals and straw purchases. Subjects were charged with violation of Title 18, United States Code, Sections 1344 (bank fraud) and 1343 (wire fraud). On 10/06/2005, six individuals were indicted and six complaints were filed. On 10/07/2005, seven complaints were filed against subjects in this case, and on 10/13/2005, an additional complaint was filed.

Operation Broken Loan was initiated to target widespread fraud in the home mortgage industry in the Detroit metropolitan area. Detroit successfully utilized a Title III in this investigation and made controlled purchases of real estate. The investigation confirmed that dishonest mortgage brokers were creating fraudulent W-2s, paycheck stubs, and employment verifications in order to qualify straw buyers for real estate purchases. The victim lenders relied on inflated appraisals and borrower certifications arranged by subjects.

CHALANA MCFARLAND (Atlanta): This case involves a mortgage fraud property flip scheme which operated from the summer of 1999 through March 2004. This case was worked by the FBI, HUD-OIG, and USPIS.

Chalana McFarland was an attorney who operated her own law firm. She acted as a title agent for title insurance companies as well as the closing attorney for various lenders.

McFarland used the stolen identity of numerous victims to submit false fraudulent loan applications. Appraisals were inflated and straw buyers were used to complete the fraudulent sales of over 100 properties. McFarland paid her identity thief $10,000 per stolen identity, as well as paying the appraiser who inflated property values over $400,000. Fraudulently obtained mortgages valued in excess of $20 million with losses in excess of $12 million.

McFarland and 16 other subjects were indicted. Fifteen

have been sentenced, with McFarland receiving 30 years in prison—the largest sentence ever for Mortgage Fraud.

THOMAS FAUNTLEROY/DAVID BOWIE (Newark): This case involves the subjects' alleged inducement of the FHA to insure mortgage loans valued over $1 million, made by Neighborhood Mortgage (owned by Bowie) to unqualified buyers. In support of the FHA loan applications, the defendants allegedly created and submitted false and fictitious bank statements, leases, IRS Forms W-2, verifications of past mortgage payments, pay stubs, attorney escrow letters, gift letters, verifications of employment, deposit checks, and fraudulent property appraisals.

To date, the following have occurred: one complaint, three informations, two indictments, three arrests, four federal convictions, and one state conviction.

MARK YOUNG (Nevada): This case involves a former Nevada First Residential Mortgage Company branch manager (Young) who directed loan officers and processors in the origination of 233 fraudulent FHA loans valued at over $25 million. Young conspired with other mortgage company employees and with employees of General Realty to manufacture and submit false employment and income documentation for borrowers. Most of the borrowers were illegal immigrants from Mexico. To date, 58 loans with a total value of $6.2 million have gone into default, with a loss to HUD of over $1.9 million. The Nevada First Residential Mortgage Company is no longer in business.

On 09/01/2005, Mark Young was found guilty on 32 counts of submitting false information to HUD, and one count of conspiracy. This case was jointly investigated by FBI,

HUD-OIG, and the Nevada Mortgage Fraud Task Force.

RANDALL DAVIDSON ET AL (Cincinnati): Randall Davidson used his companies Knab Mortgage and Capital Properties to commit Mortgage Fraud. He used unsuspecting buyers from Pittsburgh, Pennsylvania, for the purchase of depressed properties in the Dayton, Ohio, area. These properties were purchased at an inflated rate using falsified documents to secure the loans. Davidson maintained a business office in both Pittsburgh as well as Dayton. The closing agent would disburse funds prior to receiving the down payment checks in order to provide Davidson and other co-schemers with money. The closing agent was aware that many of the documents used in order to secure the loans were falsified, but continued to close the loans. Davidson would inevitably receive a large cash profit during the disbursement of funds. Currently the known loss is over $8 million. This case was jointly investigated by FBI and IRS-CID.

ROBERT A. AMICO ET AL (Buffalo): Robert A. Amico and his sons Robert J. Amico and Richard Amico engaged in a large conspiracy with loan brokers, appraisers, and buyers to submit over 100 fraudulent mortgage applications that overstated the value of all houses so that no down payment was made and so that the buyers could qualify for loans that they could not otherwise afford. All of the conspirators plead guilty, with the exception of the Amicos. Some of these conspirators were sentenced to probation and testified at the Amicos trial. Others were sentenced to jail terms of up to five years. After a six month jury trial the Amico sons were convicted and the father died of cancer. Fraudulently obtained mortgage applications were valued at $58 million with losses totaling $14.7 million. Robert J.

Amico was sentenced to 17 years in prison and Richard N. Amico was sentenced to 9 years in prison. This case was joint investigation with IRS/CID.

OPERATION CLEAN DEED (Charlotte): Promoters and other industry professionals obtained/brokered loans based on inflated property values and false application information for recruited buyer/investors. Participating attorneys falsified closing documents showing non-existent down-payments and closed the sales as "primary residence" purchases rather than as investments. The excess amount of the inflated loan was diverted to the promoters and other co-conspirators with a payment typically made to the buyer/investor following the closing. Loan payments were not made and houses eventually went into foreclosure. Fraudulently obtained loans valued in excess of $71 million with losses in excess of $9.5 million. To date, 14 subjects have been convicted, including promoters, attorneys, mortgage brokers, and builders.

AMERIFUNDING (Denver): This joint investigation with IRS/CID involved kiting of mortgage loans by utilizing stolen identities to facilitate the scheme. Further investigation determined that the scheme involved over $200 million in fraudulent loans over a 24 month period. One of the subjects obtained fraudulent identities by placing "help wanted" advertisements in a local newspaper. Information from the victims applications were used to apply for mortgage loans between $300,000 and $500,000. The proceeds of the scheme were used to pay personal expenses of the defendants. In a related fraud scheme, the lead defendant paid prior loans and purchased defective properties that were then resold for a substantial profit with inflated appraisals. To date, six subjects have been indicted.

Losses totaled $37.5 million and approximately $16 million in assets were seized.

DOTTY PIERRE ET AL (Boston): Four individuals were indicted with Bank Fraud and Aggravated Identity Theft in connection with a scheme involving the use of stolen identities to obtain mortgage loans. The subjects used stolen identity information to obtain, or attempt to obtain, mortgages worth over $800,000. This case was a joint investigation with the Postal Inspection Service, and Massachusetts State Police.

CHAPTER 9
THE CAMPAIGN TRAIL

The deeper I delve into the conspiracy, the longer the trail of corruption goes. In my opinion it leads all the way to the top of the food chain. The white house is clearly aware of the problems in the lending industry, yet doesn't take a firm stand to put an end to it. There's overwhelming evidence that our government is corruptly tied to the banking industry. The following article about the Lippo Bank speaks devastating volumes about who has the power in their pocket.

James Riady Pleads Guilty Will Pay Largest Fine in Campaign Finance History for Violating Federal Election Law

WASHINGTON, D.C. - James Tjahaja Riady will pay a record $8.6 million in criminal fines and plead guilty to a felony charge of conspiring to defraud the United States by unlawfully reimbursing campaign donors with foreign corporate funds in violation of federal election law, the Justice Department's Campaign Financing Task Force and the United States Attorney in Los Angeles announced today.

In addition, LippoBank California, a California state-chartered bank affiliated with Lippo Group, will plead guilty to 86 misdemeanor counts charging its agents, Riady and John Huang, with making illegal foreign campaign contributions from 1988 through 1994.

Riady is one of 26 people and two corporations charged by the Campaign Financing Task Force, which was established four years ago by Attorney General Janet Reno to investigate allegations of campaign financing abuses in the 1996 election cycle.

Under the terms of the plea agreement, filed today in U.S. District Court in Los Angeles, Riady, a citizen of the Republic of Indonesia, will surrender himself to the jurisdiction of the court, despite the lack of an extradition treaty between the United States and Indonesia. Once he surrenders himself, Riady will then plead guilty to the felony charge contained within the information, enter a plea on behalf of LippoBank to the 86 misdemeanor charges contained within the information, pay $8,610,000 in fines levied against himself and LippoBank, and cooperate with the government's investigation.

The $8.6 million fine represents the largest sanction imposed in a campaign finance matter in the history of the United States.

Under the agreement, Riady will continue cooperating with authorities. Since August 2000, Riady has participated in approximately a half dozen proffer sessions with government prosecutors and agents. He will be required to appear before other investigatory agencies.

In addition, Riady will waive his statutory right to apply for reentry into the U.S. for a period of two years, except when his presence is requested by the government consistent with the cooperation provisions of the plea agreement. He will also perform 400 hours of community service, forfeit to the U.S. Treasury any refunds issued to him from any political campaign committees in the wake of this announcement, and be barred from making, reimbursing or directing any future campaign contributions in U.S. elections.

The information alleges that between May 1990 and June 1994, Riady and Huang conspired to obstruct the Federal Election Commission by surreptitiously reimbursing political campaign contributions with funds often obtained from foreign individuals and entities which were prohibited sources under the Federal Election Campaign Act (FECA), and in violation of the dollar limitations established by the FECA.

According to the information, the reimbursements were accomplished through the following mechanisms:

• During the period of May 1990 through July 1991, contributions made by Huang and various employees of LippoBank from 1988 through 1991 were reimbursed with funds wired from a foreign Lippo Group entity into an account maintained by Huang at a bank in Hong Kong;

• During the period of August 1992 through October 1992, shortly after Riady pledged $1 million in support of Arkansas Governor Bill Clinton's campaign for the Presidency of the United States, contributions made by Huang were reimbursed with funds wired from a foreign Lippo Group entity into an account Riady maintained at LippoBank and then distributed to Huang in cash.

• During the period of August 1992 through September 1993, contributions made by Lippo Group entities operating in the United States were reimbursed with wire transfers from foreign Lippo Group entities.

- During the period of October 1992 through May 1994, contributions made by a Lippo Group executive were reimbursed by cash in Hong Kong.
- During the period of January 1993 through February 1994, contributions made by Huang and various Lippo Group and Lippo Bank employees were reimbursed through a fictitious "bonus" issued to Huang from a foreign Lippo Group entity.

The purpose of the contributions was to obtain various benefits from various campaign committees and candidates for Lippo Group and LippoBank, including:

- access, meetings, and time with politicians, elected officials, and other high-level government officials;
- contacts and status for Lippo Group and Lippo Bank with business and government leaders in the United States and abroad;
- business opportunities for Lippo Group and defendant LippoBank;
- government policies which would inure to the benefit of Lippo Group and defendant Lippo Bank, including Most Favored Nation status for China, open trade policies with Indonesia, normalization of relations with Vietnam, Community Reinvestment Act exemptions for LippoBank, a repeal of the Glass-Steagall Act which limited business opportunities for Lippo Bank, and a relaxation of Taiwanese restrictions on investment by foreign banks;
- the deposit of funds into Lippo Bank by political campaign committees and government agencies; and
- local government support for Lippo Group's California property development projects which would in turn benefit Lippo Bank's plans for expansion.

The unlawful conduct described in the information occurred prior to Lippo Bank's acquisition by First Bank's America, Inc. on or about March 1, 2000. First Bank's America, Inc. had no involvement in the conduct which forms the basis of the information and plea.

In addition to Riady and Lippo Bank California, the Task Force has prosecuted 25 individuals and one corporation for offenses relating to violations of the campaign financing laws.

On June 21, 2000, Pornipol "Pauline" Kanchanalak pled guilty to conspiracy to cause false statements to be made to the FEC and to causing a foreign corporation to make an illegal contribution. On that same day, codefendant Duagnet Kronenberg pled guilty to violating campaign finance laws.

On June 2, 2000, David Chang, a member of the 1996 Robert G. Torricelli Campaign Finance Committee, pled guilty to violating federal election law by making illegal contributions to the 1996 campaign of Senator Robert Torricelli. He also pled guilty to witness tampering in connection with the campaign financing task force investigation. On June 6, 2000, Chang's codefendant, Audrey Yu, pled guilty to obstruction of justice under the same superseding indictment.

On June 1, 2000, Cha-Kuek Koo, a New Jersey businessman, pled guilty to violating federal election law by making illegal contributions to the Senator Robert G. Torricelli Campaign. Koo admitted to assisting David Chang in making conduit contributions using Koo's employees at LG Group, Executive Office of the Americas. Koo's sentencing has been set for September 7, 2000.

On April 5, 2000, a federal grand jury indicted two Buddhist nuns, Venerables Yi Chu and Man Ho, with contempt of court for failing to appear as witnesses in the government's criminal trial against Maria Hsia. Yi Chu and Man Ho remain fugitives.

On March 2, 2000, Maria Hsia was convicted in D.C. on charges of causing false statements to be submitted to the FEC. The trial had been postponed pending an appeal of a ruling by the U.S. District Court in Washington, D.C., which had dismissed some of the false statement counts. In May 1999, the U.S. Court of Appeals in Washington, D.C. overturned the ruling and reinstated those counts. The task force dismissed a second indictment on tax charges after a jury in Los Angeles failed to reach a verdict. Hsia awaits sentencing.

On December 17, 1999, Yogesh Gandhi was sentenced to one year in prison for mail fraud, tax evasion, and violating federal election laws by aiding and abetting the making of a political campaign contribution by a foreign national.

On November 1, 1999, Yah Lin "Charlie" Trie, a Little Rock, Arkansas businessman, was sentenced, after pleading guilty, to a two-count information filed in Little Rock, Arkansas, to three years probation, four months home detention, 200 hours of community service, and a $5,000 fine for violating federal campaign finance laws by making political contributions in someone else's name and by causing a false statement to be made the FEC. Antonio

Pan was also indicted with Trie in the District of Columbia, but has not yet been prosecuted because he has remained outside the United States.

On September 15, 1999, Lawrence Penna, the former President of a now-defunct New Jersey securities firm, was charged with violating election laws by funneling illegal campaign contributions to the 1996 federal election campaigns of President Clinton and Senator Torricelli. Penna's case was transferred by agreement to the Southern District of New York where charges relating to his violation of United States' securities laws were pending.

On August 16, 1999, a federal judge sentenced Robert S. Lee to three years of probation and 250 hours of community service for aiding and abetting the making of an illegal foreign campaign contribution to the Democratic National Committee.

On August 12, 1999, former Lippo Executive John Huang pleaded guilty to a felony charge, filed in U.S. District Court in Los Angeles that he conspired with other employees of the Indonesia-based Lippo Group to make campaign contributions and reimburse employees with corporate funds or with funds from Indonesia. He was sentenced to one year of probation, 500 hours of community service, a $10,000 fine and directed by the judge to continue cooperating with the investigation as a condition of his probation.

On May 27, 2000, Berek Don, former GOP party leader in Bergen County, NJ, pleaded guilty to another conduit contribution scheme to the Senator Torricelli Campaign. Don awaits sentencing. On October 13, 2000 Carmine

Alampi, a Bergen County New Jersey attorney, pleaded guilty to the same scheme and was fined $5000. He also awaits sentencing.

On March 23, 1999, Juan C. Ortiz, the Chief Financial Officer of Future Tech International, Inc., was sentenced to two years probation, $20,000 in fines, and 200 hours in community service for acting as a conduit for an illegal campaign contribution and participating in the reimbursement of eight other conduit contributions.

On December 14, 1998, Johnny Chung was sentenced to probation and 3,000 hours of community service for bank fraud, tax evasion and two misdemeanor counts of conspiring to violate election law.

On November 24, 1998, Howard Glicken, a fund-raiser for the Democratic Party, was sentenced to 18 months probation, an $80,000 fine, and ordered to perform 500 hours of community service for violating campaign finance laws.

On November 4, 1998, Franklin Haney was indicted on more than 40 counts, including among others, conspiring with another to defraud the United States by impairing and impeding the FEC and conspiring to violate specific provisions of federal election law. He was acquitted of all charges on June 30, 1999.

On September 30, 1998, Democratic fund-raiser Mark B. Jimenez was indicted in Washington, D.C. on 17 counts of organizing, making and concealing illegal conduit contributions to a number of Democratic campaigns, including the Torricelli Campaign. In December 1998,

Future Tech International, Jimenez's Miami based computer sales company, pleaded guilty to tax offenses resulting from its illegal deduction of a $100,000 contribution to the DNC and employee campaign contributions reimbursed through the company's payroll. On April, 15, 1999, Jimenez, who is now in the Philippines, was indicted in Miami on additional charges of tax evasion and fraud. The task force is pursuing Jimenez's extradition from the Philippines.

In 1997, the Task Force obtained guilty pleas from Democratic fund-raisers Nora and Gene Lum, and their daughter Trisha, and Michael Brown for illegal fund-raising activities after their cases were referred from Independent Counsel Daniel Pearson. In August 1998, Gene Lum pleaded guilty to filing a false 1994 tax return and falsely preparing Nora's 1994 tax return. After cooperating with the government, he was sentenced in June 1999, to two years in prison. Nora was sentenced to 5 months in a halfway house, 5 months in home detention, and ordered to pay a $30,000 fine. Trisha Lum and Michael Brown each received probation, a $5,000 fine, costs of more than $7,000, and were ordered to perform 150 hours of community service.

Source: U.S. Department of Justice (www.usdoj.gov)

Ohio Senate vs. Ohio House

Of course, there is no lack of elected officials declaring these practices are an outrage. But for all the chest pounding, there doesn't seem to be any action being taken. This schism between talking the walk and walking the talk was painfully evident in Columbus, Ohio. The foreclosure rate in the Buckeye State is more than three times the average in the rest of the country (3.2% versus 1%). In the spring of 2006, the Ohio Senate responded by putting forth a bill that would crack down on predatory lending. But when the bill was sent to the Ohio House, they wrote in loopholes that enabled brokers to keep swindling borrowers – they even went so far as to point out how lenders could get around the bill's prohibitions.

Case in point: while the bill prohibits banks from coercing an appraiser to falsely inflate the value of a property (which is a clever way that the lender makes more money while the borrower is stuck with a debt that is greater than the value of their home), it explains how lenders can alter a house's appraised value after the fact.

Ohio House leaders claim that they are just as passionate about creating stronger consumer protection, but that the Senate's bill made strokes that were too broad.

Now this is where the fun starts. On the outside, it looks like the Senate and the House are going to duke it out in a battle royale – the House fighting for the banks, the Senate for the consumer. But when you look more closely, you realize that neither bill provides the level of advocacy one would like to see from their elected officials.

For example, the Senate bill has several restrictions which apply to financial institutions "other than banks." I believe that all financial institutions should be required to play by the same laws and regulations – especially banks.

The Senate version also instructs lenders to look out for the best interest of borrowers whose net worth is less than $25,000. This absolutely astounds me. Shouldn't they be trying to protect *everyone*? What does that say, that if a person can afford to be cheated they should be? A person's net worth should have no bearing on whether or not it is legal to rob them.

Additionally, the Senate bill restricts the amount consumers can recover in a lawsuit to their out of pocket expenses. In my opinion, the penalty for taking advantage of borrowers should be so severe that lending institutions would actually fear breaking the law. I would suggest very stiff fines and the possibility of jail time.

No Protection, No Justice

I think it's clear that while politicians spend a great deal of time pretending to do something about all the corruption, at the end of the day the consumer winds up with nothing. No protection, and certainly no justice.

What it really boils down to is money. Money dictates what laws will be written and what laws will be stricken. So if you have the money you make the laws. It's always been that way, and as far as I can tell it always will be.

And who has the most money? The banks. So just how powerful are they? The associated press ran a story about banks and credit unions which showed that in the first half of 1997, special interest groups paid $100 million *a month* on federal lobbying expenses. Whatever happened to the *common* good? Below is a perfect example from the web site www.opensecrets.org

<u>Membership Has Its Privileges</u>

Banks and credit unions are engaged in a heated battle on Capitol Hill over restrictions on federal credit union membership. A 1934 law restricts credit union membership to people who share a common employer or limited geographic area. In 1982, the National Credit Union Administration (NCUA) ruled that credit unions could open their doors to members from other businesses, organizations, and areas to help them cope with the recession. Banks argue the 1934 law makes this ruling illegal. The fight went all the way to the Supreme Court, where five justices recently ruled that NCUA's decision was "contrary to the unambiguously expressed intent of Congress." The gauntlet was thrown to Congress where Rep. Steve LaTourette (R-Ohio) has sponsored a bill, H.R. 1151, overturning the Supreme Court's decision.

The House Banking Committee held hearings on the legislation last week. Credit unions argue that allowing them to broaden their membership to people who work for different employers is key to the survival of their industry and vital to the financially disadvantaged who benefit from their lower rates and fees. Witnesses said that with 63 percent of U.S workers employed by businesses with fewer than 500 employees -- the minimum required to start a credit union -- six out of 10 workers could be denied access to credit unions. Banks counter credit unions not only break the law when they expand their membership bases, but that many have grown so large they should be taxed like other financial institutions. As non-profit cooperatives, credit unions are not taxed -- which banks say give the unions a $1 billion a year windfall. LaTourette's bill may be attached to legislation overhauling the financial services industry or pushed on its own in the coming weeks.

Commercial and savings banks have contributed $5 million in PAC and individual contributions to federal candidates so far in the 1997-98 election cycle, 67 percent to Republicans. The credit union industry has given nearly $374,000 to federal candidates, 53 percent to Republicans. The two main trade groups for the industries, the American

Bankers Association and the Credit Union National Association, spent $1.7 million and nearly $417,000 on lobbying expenses respectively in the first six months of 1997.

Top Ten House Recipients of Banks PAC & Individual Contributions, 1997-98 Election Cycle*

1. $68,000 Richard H. Baker (R-La)
2. $62,841 Bill McCollum (R-Fla)
3. $53,705 Rick A. Lazio (R-NY)
4. $49,350 Bob Riley (R-Ala)
5. $47,561 Pete Sessions (R-Texas)
6. $37,850 Jim Bunning (R-Ky)
7. $35,500 Deborah Pryce (R-Ohio)
7. $35,500 Richard A. Gephardt (D-Mo)
9. $35,050 John R. Kasich (R-Ohio)
10. $35,000 Martin Frost (D-Texas)

* Based on data downloaded from the Federal Election Commission on 3/1/98.

To me, the thing that is most frightening in this entire article is that Congress overturned the Supreme Court's decision. We are not safe people. There is nowhere to go when not even the U.S. Supreme Court can protect us. He who has the money makes the rules – and that's a terrifying truth to discover in a country that is supposed to be the guardian of civil liberty.

Below is another article posted on www.opensecrets.org which should be a wake up call for all of us.

The Banking Industry and Political Contributions

The banking industry has distributed $8.4 million in PAC and individual contributions to federal campaigns so far this cycle, 65 percent to Republicans. Credit unions have made more than $618,000 in PAC and individual contributions to federal campaigns, 54 percent to Republicans. Chairman of the Senate Banking Committee Alfonse D'Amato (R-NY) is the top Senate recipient of both industries donations over the last three election cycles. Two other Banking Committee members, Sen. Lauch Faircloth (R-NC) and Sen. Phil Gramm (R-Texas) are also top recipients of credit union and banking industry donations.

Top Senate Recipients of Bank PAC & Individual Contributions, 1993-1998*

Rank	Senator	Total
1	Alfonse M. D'Amato (R-NY)	$791,418
2	Kay Bailey Hutchison (R-Texas)	$524,622
3	Phil Gramm (R-Texas)	$414,506
4	Lauch Faircloth (R-NC)	$371,088
5	Richard C. Shelby (R-Ala)	$329,258
6	William V Roth Jr (R-Del)	$220,749
7	Bill Frist (R-Tenn)	$213,337
8	Richard G. Lugar (R-Ind)	$183,120
9	Arlen Specter (R-Pa)	$179,150
10	Robert F. Bennett (R-Utah)	$173,917

*1997-98 contributions are based on data downloaded from the FEC on 7/1/98. (Since only a third of the Senate is up every election cycle, using data from 1993 to the present captures all senators regardless when they ran for office.)

Top Senate Recipients of Credit Union PAC & Individual Contributions, 1993-1998*

Rank	Senator	Total

1	Alfonse M. D'Amato (R-NY)	$19,700
2	Lauch Faircloth (R-NC)	$16,750
3	Conrad Burns (R-Mont)	$14,000
4	Richard Bryan (D-Nev)	$12,675
5	Phil Gramm (R-Texas)	$12,500
6	Paul S. Sarbanes (D-Md)	$12,499
7	Connie Mack (R-Fla)	$11,750
8	Charles S. Robb (D-Va)	$11,000
8	Max Baucus (D-Mont)	$11,000
8	Olympia J Snowe (R-Maine)	$11,000

*1997-98 contributions are based on data downloaded from the FEC on 7/1/98.

PRESIDENT GEORGE W. BUSH

Top Contributors

MBNA Corp	$240,675
Vinson & Elkins	$202,850
Credit Suisse First Boston	$191,400
Ernst & Young	$179,949
Andersen Worldwide	$145,650
Morgan Stanley Dean Witter & Co	$144,900
Merrill Lynch	$132,425
PricewaterhouseCoopers	$127,798
Baker & Botts	$116,121
Citigroup Inc	$114,300
Goldman Sachs Group	$113,999
Enron Corp	$113,800
Bank of America	$112,500
KPMG LLP	$107,744
Jenkens & Gilchrist	$105,450
Enterprise Rent-A-Car	$97,498
State of Texas	$87,254
American General Corp	$84,134
Deloitte & Touche	$81,600
AXA Financial	$79,725

As you can see, the conspiracy goes all the way up to the top of the ladder. We are not safe from these corrupt practices. Banks are among the highest political contributors today, and they're not about to stop. Where do they get the money for such disguised payouts? The answer is simple: *you*.

Who can we trust? Who will help put an end to this illegal corruption? And corruption in the lending industry isn't limited to home loans – credit card companies are in on it too.

Campaign Contributions Made by Credit Card Banks

Americans have no one to blame but themselves for the outrageous interest rates and fees associated with credit cards. Why? Because most Americans don't bother to vote and 90% of incumbent senators and representatives are elected year after year. While Americans are sitting on the sidelines, credit card companies are lobbying Congress and contributing heavily to election campaign funds.

It shouldn't surprise you that Republicans receive more campaign contributions from the banking industry than Democrats do since the former tend to support business-friendly legislation more than the latter. It also shouldn't surprise you that the largest single corporate donor to George Bush's 2000 election campaign was a credit card company, MBNA.

In elections held from 2000 to 2004, the top ten credit card companies contributed the following amounts to various campaigns (amounts are rounded, in millions). These amounts do not include the millions they spend on lobbyists. Note that federal legislation limits the amount corporations can give to candidates.

Company	Republicans	Democrats
MBNA	$5.2	$1.1
Citigroup	$4.5	$4.3
Discover (Morgan Stanley)	$3.5	$2.2
Bank One	$1.9	$1.3
Bank of America	$1.8	$1.7
Household (HSEC)	$1.4	$0.7
American Express	$1.2	$0.9
Chase (JP Morgan)	$1.1	$1.0
Capital One	$0.7	$0.2
Providian	$0.5	$0.5

Source: www.bcsalliance.com.

CHAPTER 10
IT'S ALL ABOUT THE MONEY

In the end, we're talking about money: your money, the bank's money, the broker's money, the REALTOR®'s money, and the politician's money. There's lot of money changing hands, but the truth is that it all starts with you and your loan. Most people overlook this very important part of the puzzle:

It is all about you and your money

How much can they get from you? That depends on how eager you are to get your loan, and to what lengths you are willing to go to get it. I cannot think of a broker who really puts you above everything else. I'm sometimes doubtful that your needs even figure into their equation. But then, why would they have to?

I'm a REALTOR®, which means that even when I'm hired I'm not required. What I mean is that many people buy and sell homes on their own without a real estate agent to help them. But when it comes to the loan, you always need a broker or a banker to step in and fund the deal. They know this, and use that information to their benefit.

There are great differences in the regulations between bankers and REALTOR®s, the biggest being disclosure. Bankers are not required to disclose how much money they make off of your loan. They could be making three percentage points on the back end of the loan and not even tell you. Imagine having a $450,000 loan and finding out that your banker made $13,500 from you at closing. And what does that really cost you? Let's see... if you have a 30 year loan at 6.5% interest, then that $13,500 is going to cost you $877.50 per year in interest. Multiply that by 30 years and you get $26,325. Add that to the original $13,500 paid to the broker, and your total cost is $39,825! For most people, that's more than a full year's salary. No wonder these figures aren't disclosed – if they were, most people would insist on renegotiating their loan.

Who is to Blame?

May I have the envelope please? And the answer is…

We all are.

Yes, the politicians are corrupt. Yes, the banks and mortgage brokers are greedy. But we as consumers and voters let them get away with it. Still, some of us are guiltier then others. So let's break it down.

Problems with Brokers

If I had to name one party as the biggest culprit in this whole mess, the choice would be pretty clear: it's the broker. We go to them with the intent of getting help, and we leave with the promise that we will get just that. The broker then turns around and auctions our needs to the highest bidder. And they're so greedy that getting kickbacks from banks isn't enough. They still hit us up with all kinds of garbage fees to increase their profits.

Part of the problem is that the requirements for becoming a broker are so easy that just about anyone can do it. But if there were to be greater requirements for joining the profession – including a longer time in the field as an apprentice – then I believe the amount of fraud would be greatly reduced.

But the biggest problem with brokers today is that they have no loyalty to their client's best interests. They are only looking out for their own well being. The broker should hold up to their agreement of implied employment when they are hired to seek out a loan for their client.

Printed below are some headlines that support my opinion of mortgage brokers.

Ameriquest Settlement Worries Brokers
WASHINGTON -- The chairman of a mortgage broker trade group warned that the landmark settlement reached earlier this year with Ameriquest Mortgage Co. has big implications for mortgage brokers.

Plot Thickens at Class Action Law Firm
A retired mortgage broker has admitted he was illegally paid millions of dollars by a major law firm that has filed numerous class-action lawsuits against large lenders.

IL Sues Mortgage Companies for Fraud
The Illinois Attorney General has filed two lawsuits against three companies she says claim to help homeowners facing foreclosure keep their houses but that actually engage in mortgage rescue fraud.

Lawsuit Suggests Ameriquest Shouldn't Have Made Loan
Ameriquest Mortgage Co. is facing a lawsuit filed in Utah's federal court brought by an elderly woman who claims company representatives cajoled her into obtaining a loan at double the interest rate she could have gotten from her

credit union. But the subprime lender sees no merit in her allegations.

Ocwen Hit with Biggest Judgment Ever

A Texas attorney has handed Florida-based Ocwen Financial Corp. a one-two punch by obtaining the two largest legal verdicts ever against the company.

Mortgage Company Loses Lawsuit

A Colorado court has ruled against a mortgage company that allegedly deceived delinquent borrowers into giving up their homes.

Source: www/mortgagedaily.com

Problems with Lenders

When it comes to lenders, many servicing companies are guilty of corruption as well.

Several Class Actions Filed Against MD Lenders

One of Maryland's most prominent class action attorneys has trained his sights on mortgage lenders in Maryland, setting up a predatory lending unit within his law firm, running newspaper ads and accusing an increasing number of lenders in court of charging excessive and illegal fees. But Maryland lenders and mortgage associations say the lawsuits have no merit and will hurt consumers and the smaller mortgage lenders.

Source: www.mortgagedaily.com

Problems with Everyone Else

Next in line are the politicians. They are so corrupt that they'd need the world's largest warehouse to store all of their dirty little secrets. If I had a penny for every dollar politicians made illegally, I'd be the richest person to date. There are so many illegal campaigns being run that if you removed every dishonest person from office, it would be impossible for our government to function.

Then come the banks and servicing companies with their hidden agendas, followed by the dishonest appraisers, the crooked home inspectors, the overpriced insurance companies, and the occasional REALTOR® who just wants to make a sale.

Mortgages can be hazardous to your financial health because the majority of consumers just don't know any better. You, like me, prefer to assume that everyone is on the up and up. You go out with the excitement we all have when we buy or sell, and trust that you are in good hands. Well, guess again my friend. You're not!

Who is to blame? We all are.

Which leaves one simple question:

What are you going to do about it?

CHAPTER 11
Was I Cheated?

By now you're probably asking yourself, "was I cheated?" Depending on who you ask, you're going to get a different answer. Here's mine:

If you currently have a home loan, if you have ever had a home loan, or if you have refinanced an existing home loan, then I would say that the chances you were cheated are 90% or greater. But that's my opinion. Many people have a different outlook on the same set of circumstances.

And by that I mean this: it's a fact that brokers and lenders withhold information. It's a fact that you are not given full disclosure. It's a fact that you do not see their bottom line. Fact, fact, fact. I look at this information and I see behavior which is duplicitous, deceitful, and ultimately cheating you out of your money. But there are others who would argue that this is acceptable behavior; that their withholding information is okay. They call it business, I call it a lie.

So rather than argue ethics, I would pose a question of logistics: would the information that is being hidden from us change the way we do business, and would it have a factor on whether or not we choose to do business with that company or any other company? In my opinion, the answer would be "yes".

Here's an analogy that I think most sane people would agree with. If you were to buy a loaf of bread only to find that it had mold in it, would you bring it back to where you purchased it and complain? Would you want your money back? What if the store personnel said that you had asked for bread, and bread is what they gave you? What if they said you did not ask for *fresh* bread, and that they are not required to refund your money? Would that make them right? The obvious answer here is that you were expecting what every other consumer is expecting: a fresh loaf of bread.

The problem with mortgages is that in most cases you automatically assume that your best interests are being looked after. You expect that the broker's one goal is serving your needs. Such is usually not the case. Most people think that getting a loan is more important than knowing what type of loan they are getting and what that loan is going to cost them.

It is important to know what questions to ask your broker or lender. It is very important to understand all the fees that are involved with your loan. It is important for you, the borrower, to understand how your broker is paid, because that could mean a difference in thousands of dollars over the term of the loan. When I asked my broker to explain how he made money off my loan, I was flat out lied to. The sad part is not that the broker was my friend (which he was), nor that I lost a lot of money (which I did). The sad part is that I am a REALTOR®, and I should have known better.

Unfortunately, real estate school doesn't teach home loans or lending practices. It is sad to say that REALTOR®s are considered professionals in the field of real estate, yet when it comes to the most important part of buying a home – the loan – our education is limited at best. Let me say that again: **the most important part of buying a home is the loan, and REALTOR®s are not taught anything about them.**

I asked, "Why is this not taught in real estate school? Why isn't this information required for our licensing?" And I was answered, "We are not required to know lending laws. We are not in the business of doing loans."

But I was taught that our job is to help our clients buy and sell their homes and protect them in all related negotiations. Doesn't that include the loan? If REALTOR® fees are negotiable and the home sale price is negotiable, then surely the brokerage fees are negotiable as well. Your REALTOR® is hired to help you negotiate these items while protecting your best interests.

What ever happened to the words "Truth in Lending?" Does the idea still exist? We live in a world with so many rules and regulations that I would think that owning a home – which is one of the biggest parts of your life – would be closely regulated to protect you from unscrupulous lending practices. But the companies behind this crime are among the biggest campaign contributors and lobbyists in the government today. Banking and commerce drive this country. They put politicians in office to keep these very practices alive and thriving.

What we can do is band together and insist that our politicians change these laws and make sure that all fees and payouts to all parties are clearly explained and shown for all people to see and understand. I am surprised that some fast acting aggressive law firm has not already filed a class action lawsuit to penalize these lenders and brokers that allow such dishonest unfair practices to go on.

Were you cheated? The answer is that you probably were. Is there an easy way to determine the extent? The answer to that question is not always as easy. In some cases it is clear cut and obvious, as shown in the graph of the HUD Settlement Statement below. The circled area marks hidden, excess fees.

L. Settlement Charges				Paid From Borrowers Funds at Settlement	Paid From Seller's Funds at Settlement
700. Total Sales/Broker's Commission based on price $244,900.00 @ 6% = $14,694.00					
Division of Commission (line 700) as follows:					
701.	$7,347.00	to	Listing Agent		
702.	$7,347.00	to	Buyers Agent		
703. Commission paid at Settlement					
704.					$14,694.00
800. Items Payable In Connection With Loan					
801. Loan Origination Fee		%			
802. Loan Discount		%			
803. Appraisal Fee		to			
804. Credit Report		to	Mortgage Company	$12.39	
805. Lender's Inspection Fee				$650.00	
806. Mortgage Insurance Application Fee to					
807. Assumption Fee					
808. Processing Fee To: Mortgage Company				$995.00	
809. Administration Fee To: Mortgage Company				$2,204.00	
810. Premium Paid By Lender To: Mortgage Company			$6,612.00		
811. Tax To : Lender				$70.00	

In most cases, your HUD Settlement Statement will have a section called "Items Payable in Connection With Loan", as shown in the example below.

L. Settlement Charges				Paid From Borrowers Funds at Settlement	Paid From Seller's Funds at Settlement
700. Total Sales/Broker's Commission based on price $244,900.00 @ 6% = $14,694.00					
Division of Commission (line 700) as follows:					
701.	$7,347.00	to	Listing Agent		
702.	$7,347.00	to	Buyers Agent		
703. Commission paid at Settlement					
704.					$14,694.00
800. Items Payable In Connection With Loan					
801. Loan Origination Fee		%			
802. Loan Discount		%			
803. Appraisal Fee		to			
804. Credit Report		to	Mortgage Company	$12.39	
805. Lender's Inspection Fee				$650.00	
806. Mortgage Insurance Application Fee to					
807. Assumption Fee					
808. Processing Fee To: Mortgage Company				$995.00	
809. Administration Fee To: Mortgage Company				$2,204.00	
810. Premium Paid By Lender To: Mortgage Company			$6,612.00		
811. Tax To : Lender				$70.00	
900. Items Required By Lender To Be Paid In Advance					
901. Interest from	to	@ $	/day		
902. Mortgage Insurance Premium for			months to		
903. Hazard Insurance Premium for			years to		
904.			years to		
905.					

This section lists all the expenses required to be paid in connection with your loan. If you look closely, you will often see hidden dollar amounts, like the $6,612 listed on line 810 above. Many times, these numbers are not shown. This is money that the lender has paid the broker for finding you, the borrower. Which brings us back to the question I raised in Chapter 6: isn't that being paid twice to do the same job? If so, why in hell are we paying him again if he is already being paid?

Two reasons. First, we're not supposed to *know* that he is being paid, let alone how much. Second, they are dishonest, corrupt, lying, cheating thieves.

Think back to when you first sat down with your mortgage broker and filled out your credit report and applied for a loan. After filling out all the papers and answering all the questions (which probably seemed to last for days), you finally got to discuss the loan itself. Do you remember when the broker said what your interest rate would be, and that it was based on the credit information you provided? Did the broker also explain that there are many ways to get a lower interest rate by giving you lower payments and saving you money? He didn't, did he? Here's why.

When the broker shops your loan, he is looking for the best deal for *both* you *and* himself. If he were to find you a loan that would save you a ton of money but paid him almost nothing for a finder's fee, do you think you'd ever see that loan? I doubt it.

What brokers usually do is try to find a win-win situation: the loan is agreeable to you and profitable to them. They would argue that's why they're in business, to make money. I would argue that they should not get paid twice for doing the same job. A broker's job should be to find you the best loan for your money and credit rating. It's almost as if they're working for themselves and not for you, the paying client.

If I was cheated, how much was I cheated and what can I do about it now?

Going over your HUD Settlement Statement and looking for these simple items can give you a clear understanding of where your money is going and how much you might have lost. To calculate shaved points, you might wish to seek the help of a financial or consumer credit counselor to score your credit. Many banking institutions will post this information for you if you ask. You can also have a professional review your existing loan or mortgage based on your credit rating at the time of the loan to determine if you were given the correct percentage rate. If you find discrepancies or excessive charges in your loan, you might want to consult an attorney to see if you have any legal recourse.

I challenge anyone to tell me of a single time that they went to a broker's office and had that broker turn their computer screen around while they were shopping a loan. I challenge anyone to tell me of a singe time that their broker showed them how much money lending institutions would give them, the broker, for throwing your business their way. It has never – NEVER – been done.

Another issue I want to address is theft by fraud. This type of theft usually happens with the help of your friendly neighborhood REALTOR®, and it hurts my heart to tell you how many times I see or hear it happen every day. It has to do with the appraisal of the home being sold or purchased. Oftentimes the REALTOR® and mortgage broker know that the property will not appraise at the value they require, so they use "a preferred appraiser."

A preferred appraiser is one that works with a particular broker quite often, and in return for this repeat business has been known to stretch an appraisal beyond its true value. So, for example: assume that your home is worth $450,000 and you need a loan amount to show a value of $465,000 to get the loan to value ratio in line. The broker explains to his preferred appraiser the spot he's in and requests an appraisal to equal or exceed that amount of $465,000. And voila: through magic and the appraiser's compliance, the house is now valued at $15,000 above its actual worth.

But this is terrible for the buyer, who ends up owing more than the value of his home. In this situation there are three parties at fault: your REALTOR®, your broker, and your appraiser. If you think you've been in this kind of situation, I'd recommend consulting an attorney. You might be able to seek damages.

To avoid being cheated, you should stick with reputable companies with solid references and a long history of great service. Too often there are independent, overnight start-up companies that are not widely recognized. I would recommend working with the national companies, so that if you have a problem you can expect proper attention to fixing it.

CHAPTER 12
THE SOLUTION

The solution can be laid out quite simply by reminding ourselves to slow down and read everything front to back, top to bottom, with a fine tooth comb.

If you aren't sure what you're reading, seek help from a third party. If the third party can't satisfy your questions, get a second or even a third opinion. When it comes to mortgages, you should never rush into things without double and triple checking everything. Remember: you always have the right to say "no." You always have the right to say "let me think about it." You always have the right to wait until you are comfortable with the decision you are making. And remember the old adage, "if it sounds too good to be true, it probably is."

I've always been the sort of person who rushes into things blindly with the hope that everything will work itself out on its own. I have come to learn that this strategy usually works against me, and that I should have known better. Don't let this happen to you.

Always remember that knowledge is power. If you're going to make a big decision that can affect the way you live or manage your future, then make sure you go through all the right steps.

Do your homework on the companies you're thinking about doing business with. Check with the better business bureau to see if there have been any complaints filed against them, and if there have, look at the type of complaint as well as the frequency. Always interview the companies you're considering as if your life depended on it.

Remember: you are hiring them.

I would recommend looking into companies that have been around for a long time and are nationally recognized for their service. And don't hesitate to ask for a written guarantee – if a company is not willing to back their service with a guarantee, then perhaps you should look elsewhere. Keep in mind that just because a company's been around a long time doesn't mean that the person you're dealing with has. You might want to meet with the managing broker to explain your concerns and make sure that you're working with a veteran in the field.

Look for companies that are willing to take their time with you and explain everything that you are signing. If you feel rushed in any part of the process, ask them to slow down and go over what each item is. If they try to rush you through their forms, consider it a big, red warning sign. They are being paid a great deal of money for a very short amount of time, and you are paying a great deal of money for a very long time.

I strongly recommend taking a note pad with you to write down any questions you might have or think of later, and write the answers you were given next to the question so you can check the accuracy of the answers later.

As a last resort, you might want to have an attorney that is familiar with real estate look everything over before you sign. Attorneys cost money, but it's an investment that will pay off if they catch something you have overlooked.

Finally, you may want to become an expert in the field of lending and real estate. If you know as much or more than the broker you are dealing with, it will be very hard for them to cheat you out of your hard earned money. And if all else fails, you can always pray!

Shopping Your Loan!!!

The Mortgage Brokers Treasure Hunt

So you've filled out all of your paperwork, and your mortgage broker tells you that he's out shopping your loan. There are hundreds of servicing companies available for him to choose from. But you need to understand that he will really only be taking your loan to a small handful.

Why? Two reasons:

1. It takes too much effort to become familiar with all the different terms, rates, guidelines and payout structures.

My experience is that most brokers are lazy. They don't want to do the work required to get you the very best loan. They would much rather get the easiest loan done quickly, so they can get paid as soon and as much as possible.

2. In many cases, servicing companies offer incentives for volume.

Did you know that there are web sites set up with **SECRET PASSWORDS** for mortgage brokers to shop your loan? Did you know that the main emphasis of these web sites is *how much the broker will make off of your loan*? That's right – they're not designed to show how *you* can get the best deal, but how the *broker* can make the most money.

And yet, every servicing company has a web site which is designed to give mortgage brokers up to the minute information. In many ways it's like the pit on the floor of the stock exchange – everyone is trying hard to buy and sell. If your broker wanted to, they could find you the very best deal available. They have the tools and a wide array of companies hungry to get your business.

But do they do that? No. They're looking out for what will make them the most money. Of course, they don't tell you that. When was the last time a broker said, "I think you should go with this lender because they're going to give me the sweetest deal?" Never – but I can virtually guarantee that's what's behind their recommendation.

I have a friend that's a mortgage broker, and I can't tell you how many times I've heard him brag to colleagues about how much money he's made off of various clients. One time the payoff he was bragging about seemed ridiculously big for the size of the loan. So I asked him "how did you make so much money on such a small loan?" He replied, "If I don't get it here, I'll get it there, or here, or there, or over here – but believe you me *I will get it*."

I was once privy to a loan agreement in which part of the broker's charges were $2000 for an administrative fee. How can that be possible? That particular loan made this broker a total of $9800, and he worked less than 14 hours to get it. That equates to $700 per hour. Due to legal issues, I will refrain from copying the specific information for your eyes to see. I will, however, advise you to ask your mortgage broker to show you their computer screen while they're shopping your loan, and ask for a full explanation of what you see. If he refuses, then I suggest you get up and leave. That broker's not to be trusted!

What Your Broker Sees!

On the next page is an example of what your broker would read on the website of a servicing company. The chart shows you the rate the service companies pay or charge a broker for your loan. The numbers to the right of the final rate column indicate the percentage of yield spread on the loan. For example, 2.5 means 2.5% of the total cost of your loan.

Keep in mind that if the number to the right of the final rate column is negative, the broker is receiving money at the close of escrow. If the number is positive, the broker is paying money.

With that said, we should not forget that if the broker does this online he gets a 0.5% credit on top of this chart. For example, the chart shows that a 7.000% final rate closed in 14 days yields 0.000 – nothing. But if the broker does the transaction online, he'll get 0.5%. To determine the true cash value, multiply the percentage by the total cost of the loan.

An example would be 2% x $260,000 = $5,200.

These numbers do not include garbage processing fees and origination fees that the broker charges at the front end of the loan.

Here's what they see:

THE FOLLOWING PRICING REFLECTS ALL APPLICABLE ADJUSTMENTS BASED ON THE LOAN SCENARIO AS INPUT BY USER.

WHOLESALE ACCOUNTS ONLY** you will receive a one-time additional 0.5% Yield Spread Premium if you submit your loan online, and then lock online. Findings must be received prior to locking in order to receive this incentive. *If you are viewing this message on a Lock Confirmation, any applicable incentives have already been calculated in your price* Please refer to the latest Incentive bulletin posted on the website for additional details.

Final Rate	14 Days	30 Days	45 Days	60 Days
7.750%	--	--	--	-2.500
7.625%	--	-2.500	-2.500	-2.250
7.500%	-2.500	-2.250	-2.125	-1.875
7.375%	-2.375	-2.000	-1.875	-1.625
7.250%	-2.000	-1.625	-1.500	-1.250
7.125%	-1.750	-1.375	-1.250	-1.000
7.000%	-1.500 Broker Profit	-1.125	-1.000	-0.750
6.875%	-1.125	-0.750	-0.625	-0.375
6.750%	-0.875	-0.500	-0,375	-0.125
6.625%	-0.500	-0.125	-0.000	0.250
6.500%	0.000	0.375 Broker Loss	0.500	0.750
6.375%	0.500	0.875	1.000	1.250
6.250%	1.000	1.375	1.500	1.750
6.125%	1.500	1.875	2.000	2.250
6.000%	2.000	2.375	2.500	2.750
5.875%	2.500	2.875	3.00	3.250

Looking for the Best Mortgage

Here is some of the best information I have found. It comes from the Federal Trade Commission Website (www.ftc.gov)

> Shopping around for a home loan or mortgage will help you to get the best financing deal. A mortgage—whether it's a home purchase, a refinancing, or a home equity loan—is a product, just like a car, so the price and terms may be negotiable. You will want to compare all the costs involved in obtaining a mortgage. Shopping, comparing, and negotiating may save you thousands of dollars.

> Obtain Information from Several Lenders

> Home loans are available from several types of lenders— thrift institutions, commercial banks, mortgage companies, and credit unions. Different lenders may quote you different prices, so you should contact several lenders to make sure you arere getting the best price. You can also get a home loan through a mortgage broker. Brokers arrange transactions rather than lending money directly; in other words, they find a lender for you. A broker's access to several lenders can mean a wider selection of loan products and terms from which you can choose. Brokers will generally contact several lenders regarding your application, but they are not obligated to find the best deal for you unless they have contracted with you to act as your agent. Consequently, you should consider contacting more than one broker, just as you should with banks or thrift institutions.

> Whether you are dealing with a lender or a broker may not always be clear. Some financial institutions operate as both lenders and brokers. And most brokers' advertisements do

not use the word "broker." Therefore, be sure to ask whether a broker is involved. This information is important because brokers are usually paid a fee for their services that may be separate from and in addition to the lender's origination or other fees. A broker's compensation may be in the form of "points" paid at closing or as an add-on to your interest rate, or both. You should ask each broker you work with how he or she will be compensated so that you can compare the different fees. Be prepared to negotiate with the brokers as well as the lenders.

Obtain All Important Cost Information

Be sure to get information about mortgages from several lenders or brokers. Know how much of a down payment you can afford, and find out all the costs involved in the loan. Knowing just the amount of the monthly payment or the interest rate is not enough. Ask for information about the same loan amount, loan term, and type of loan so that you can compare the information. The following information is important to get from each lender and broker:

Rates

• Ask each lender and broker for a list of its current mortgage interest rates and whether the rates being quoted are the lowest for that day or week.

• Ask whether the rate is fixed or adjustable. Keep in mind that when interest rates for adjustable-rate loans go up, generally so does the monthly payment.

• If the rate quoted is for an adjustable-rate loan, ask how your rate and loan payment will vary, including whether your loan payment will be reduced when rates go down.

- Ask about the loan's annual percentage rate (APR). The APR takes into account not only the interest rate but also points, broker fees, and certain other credit charges that you may be required to pay, expressed as a yearly rate.

Points

Points are fees paid to the lender or broker for the loan and are often linked to the interest rate; usually the more points you pay, the lower the rate.

- Check your local newspaper for information about rates and points currently being offered.

- Ask for points to be quoted to you as a dollar amount— rather than just as the number of points—so that you will actually know how much you will have to pay.

Fees

A home loan often involves many fees, such as loan origination or underwriting fees, broker fees, and transaction, settlement, and closing costs. Every lender or broker should be able to give you an estimate of its fees. Many of these fees are negotiable. Some fees are paid when you apply for a loan (such as application and appraisal fees), and others are paid at closing. In some cases, you can borrow the money needed to pay these fees, but doing so will increase your loan amount and total costs. "No cost" loans are sometimes available, but they usually involve higher rates.

- Ask what each fee includes. Several items may be lumped

into one fee.

- Ask for an explanation of any fee you do not understand. Some common fees associated with a home loan closing are listed on the Mortgage Shopping Worksheet in this brochure.

Down Payments and Private Mortgage Insurance

Some lenders require 20 percent of the home's purchase price as a down payment. However, many lenders now offer loans that require less than 20 percent down—sometimes as little as 5 percent on conventional loans. If a 20 percent down payment is not made, lenders usually require the home buyer to purchase private mortgage insurance (PMI) to protect the lender in case the home buyer fails to pay. When government-assisted programs such as FHA (Federal Housing Administration), VA (Veterans Administration), or Rural Development Services are available, the down payment requirements may be substantially smaller.

- Ask about the lender's requirements for a down payment, including what you need to do to verify that funds for your down payment are available.

- Ask your lender about special programs it may offer.

  If PMI is required for your loan,

- Ask what the total cost of the insurance will be.

- Ask how much your monthly payment will be when including the PMI premium.

• Ask how long you will be required to carry PMI.

Obtain the Best Deal That You Can

Once you know what each lender has to offer, negotiate for the best deal that you can. On any given day, lenders and brokers may offer different prices for the same loan terms to different consumers, even if those consumers have the same loan qualifications. The most likely reason for this difference in price is that loan officers and brokers are often allowed to keep some or all of this difference as extra compensation. Generally, the difference between the lowest available price for a loan product and any higher price that the borrower agrees to pay is an overage. When overages occur, they are built into the prices quoted to consumers. They can occur in both fixed and variable-rate loans and can be in the form of points, fees, or the interest rate. Whether quoted to you by a loan officer or a broker, the price of any loan may contain overages.

Have the lender or broker write down all the costs associated with the loan. Then ask if the lender or broker will waive or reduce one or more of its fees or agree to a lower rate or fewer points. You'll want to make sure that the lender or broker is not agreeing to lower one fee while raising another or to lower the rate while raising points. There's no harm in asking lenders or brokers if they can give better terms than the original ones they quoted or than those you have found elsewhere.

Once you are satisfied with the terms you have negotiated, you may want to obtain a written lock-in from the lender or broker. The lock-in should include the rate that you have agreed upon, the period the lock-in lasts, and the number of points to be paid. A fee may be charged for locking in the loan rate. This fee may be refundable at closing. Lock-ins can protect you from rate increases while your loan is being processed; if rates fall, however, you could end up with a less favorable rate. Should that happen, try to negotiate a compromise with the lender or broker.

Remember: Shop, Compare, Negotiate

When buying a home, remember to shop around, to compare costs and terms, and to negotiate for the best deal. Your local newspaper and the Internet are good places to start shopping for a loan. You can usually find information both on interest rates and on points for several lenders. Since rates and points can change daily, you'll want to check your newspaper often when shopping for a home loan. But the newspaper does not list the fees, so be sure to ask the lenders about them.

Don't be afraid to make lenders and brokers compete with each other for your business by letting them know that you are shopping for the best deal.

Fair Lending Is Required by Law

The Equal Credit Opportunity Act prohibits lenders from discriminating against credit applicants in any aspect of a credit transaction on the basis of race, color, religion, national origin, sex, marital status, age, whether all or part of the applicant's income comes from a public assistance program, or whether the applicant has in good faith exercised a right under the Consumer Credit Protection Act.

The Fair Housing Act prohibits discrimination in residential real estate transactions on the basis of race, color, religion, sex, handicap, familial status, or national origin.

Under these laws, a consumer cannot be refused a loan based on these characteristics nor be charged more for a loan or offered less favorable terms based on such characteristics.

<u>Credit Problems? Still Shop, Compare, and Negotiate</u>

Don't assume that minor credit problems or difficulties stemming from unique circumstances, such as illness or temporary loss of income, will limit your loan choices to only high-cost lenders.

If your credit report contains negative information that is accurate, but there are good reasons for trusting you to repay a loan, be sure to explain your situation to the lender or broker. If your credit problems cannot be explained, you will probably have to pay more than borrowers who have good credit histories. But don't assume that the only way to get credit is to pay a high price. Ask how your past credit history affects the price of your loan and what you would need to do to get a better price. Take the time to shop around and negotiate the best deal that you can.

Avoid Paying Closing Costs

There are a few simple ways to avoid paying closing costs *ever again*.

1. You can work with your agent to ask the seller to contribute at closing. This simply means that the seller pays your closing costs at escrow. There is usually a limit of 6% allowed to be contributed to your loan based on the lenders requirements.

2. You can have your agent and the other agent contribute to your closing costs from the proceeds of their commission. This would also be done through escrow.

3. You could work with your broker and have them pay your costs based on the type of loan you do. For example, if your broker were making two points in the back of the loan and one point in the front, it would not be too difficult to have the broker offer up a portion of their profit to help in your closing costs.

4. A combination of all the above would be a sure remedy to eliminate all closing costs.

It all boils down to negotiation and bottom line profits. It is important to understand how the loan process works and use it to your advantage. If you know that your mortgage broker is making money on the back end of your loan, then demand that they forfeit their fees on the front end. These fees would include not only origination fees but also processing and other garbage fees. It comes down to a simple case of offer and acceptance. You offer the mortgage broker a payday, but limit how much the paycheck will be. If the mortgage broker is resistant, then tell them you'll shop your loan to other brokers. I can assure you that for every broker who won't play ball, there are two who will.

Getting a Lower Interest Rate

Avoid using a mortgage broker all together and go directly to the servicer. You'll save them the cost of having to pay a brokerage fee, and that savings can be passed on to you by buying down your interest rate, lowering your closing cost, and/or eliminating some or all of your fees. Keep in mind that when you sit down with a banker, they might look at you like you're crazy. That's because you'll be the very first person they've met armed with the knowledge you now possess. And with the use of this valuable information, you'll be able to literally laugh all the way to the bank.

Use a REALTOR®

I strongly urge you to hire a REALTOR®. There are many real estate companies that offer exceptional services. I would recommend that you interview with the managing broker to see who you feel is most receptive to your needs. Remember that a real estate broker is not the same as a mortgage broker – they are two completely different things. A real estate agent is bound by a strict code of ethics (see Appendix 2); a mortgage broker is not. A national survey was recently done that showed using an agent netted sellers almost 13% more money than those home sellers not using an agent. The reason I point this out is simply that using a knowledgeable trade professional can have a positive effect. The old adage "knowledge is power" is true, and unfortunately not a lot of knowledge has been readily available to consumers with regards to loans.

Don't Be a Victim of Loan Fraud

Quoted below is an article from the U.S. Department of Housing and Urban Development (www.hud.gov).

Protect Yourself from Predatory Lenders

Buying or refinancing your home may be one of the most important and complex financial decisions you'll ever make. Many lenders, appraisers, and real estate professionals stand ready to help you get a nice home and a great loan. However, you need to understand the home buying process to be a smart consumer. Every year, misinformed homebuyers, often first-time purchasers or seniors, become victims of predatory lending or loan fraud.

Don't let this happen to you!

11 Tips on Being a Smart Consumer

1. Before you buy a home, attend a homeownership education course offered by the U.S. Department of Housing and Urban Development (HUD)-approved, non-profit counseling agencies.

2. Interview several real estate professionals (agents), and ask for and check references before you select one to help you buy or sell a home.

3. Get information about the prices of other homes in the neighborhood. Don't be fooled into paying too much.

4. Hire a properly qualified and licensed home inspector to carefully inspect the property before you are obligated to buy. Determine whether you or the seller is going to be responsible for paying for the repairs. If you have to pay for the repairs, determine whether or not you can afford to make them.

5. Shop for a lender and compare costs. Be suspicious if anyone tries to steer you to just one lender.

6. Do NOT let anyone persuade you to make a false statement on your loan application, such as overstating

your income, the source of your down payment, failing to disclose the nature and amount of your debts, or even how long you have been employed. When you apply for a mortgage loan, every piece of information that you submit must be accurate and complete. Lying on a mortgage application is fraud and may result in criminal penalties.

7.   Do NOT let anyone convince you to borrow more money than you know you can afford to repay. If you get behind on your payments, you risk losing your house and all of the money you put into your property.

8.   Never sign a blank document or a document containing blanks. If information is inserted by someone else after you have signed, you may still be bound to the terms of the contract. Insert "N/A" (i.e., not applicable) or cross through any blanks.

9.   Read everything carefully and ask questions. Do not sign anything that you don't understand. Before signing, have your contract and loan agreement reviewed by an attorney skilled in real estate law, consult with a trusted real estate professional or ask for help from a housing counselor with a HUD-approved agency. If you cannot afford an attorney, take your documents to the HUD-approved housing counseling agency near you to find out if they will review the documents or can refer you to an attorney who will help you for free or at low cost.

10.   Be suspicious when the cost of a home improvement goes up if you don't accept the contractor's

financing.

11. Be honest about your intention to occupy the house. Stating that you plan to live there when, in fact, you are not (because you intend to rent the house to someone else or fix it up and resell it) violates federal law and is a crime.

What is Predatory Lending?

In communities across America, people are losing their homes and their investments because of predatory lenders, appraisers, mortgage brokers and home improvement contractors who:

• Sell properties for much more than they are worth using false appraisals.

• Encourage borrowers to lie about their income, expenses, or cash available for down payments in order to get a loan.

• Knowingly lend more money than a borrower can afford to repay.

• Charge high interest rates to borrowers based on their race or national origin and not on their credit history.

• Charge fees for unnecessary or nonexistent products and services.

• Pressure borrowers to accept higher-risk loans such as balloon loans, interest only payments, and steep pre-payment penalties.

- Target vulnerable borrowers to cash-out refinances offers when they know borrowers are in need of cash due to medical, unemployment or debt problems.

- "Strip" homeowners' equity from their homes by convincing them to refinance again and again when there is no benefit to the borrower.

- Use high pressure sales tactics to sell home improvements and then finance them at high interest rates.

What Tactics Do Predators Use?

- A lender or investor tells you that they are your only chance of getting a loan or owning a home. You should be able to take your time to shop around and compare prices and houses.

- The house you are buying costs a lot more than other homes in the neighborhood, but is not any bigger or better.

- You are asked to sign a sales contract or loan documents that are blank or that contain information which is not true.

- You are told that the Federal Housing Administration insurance protects you against property defects or loan fraud - it does not.

- The cost or loan terms at closing are not what you agreed to.

- You are told that refinancing can solve your credit or money problems.

- You are told that you can only get a good deal on a home improvement if you finance it with a particular lender.

Final Thoughts

If a deal to buy, repair, or refinance a house sounds too good to be true, it probably is!

Oddly, this is an area where choosing someone from a referral might not be the best idea. In most cases, good service leads to referrals. But in this case, we have to assume that most people were not dealt with fairly and never even knew it.

Remember that if someone doesn't want to disclose their full earnings from your loan, they should not be trusted and I would encourage you to take your business elsewhere.

Last, but most important, remember…

NEGOTIATE, NEGOTIATE, NEGOTIATE! It is your right!

GLOSSARY

401(K)/403(B): An employer-sponsored investment plan that allows individuals to set aside tax-deferred income for retirement or emergency purposes. 401(k) plans are provided by employers that are private corporations. 403(b) plans are provided by employers that are not for profit organizations.

401(K)/403(B) LOAN: Some administrators of 401(k)/403(b) plans allow for loans against the monies you have accumulated in these plans. Loans against 401K plans are an acceptable source of down payment for most types of loans.

ACCELERATION CLAUSE: A clause in your mortgage which allows the lender to demand payment of the outstanding loan balance for various reasons. The most common reasons for accelerating a loan are if the borrower defaults on the loan or transfers title to another individual without informing the lender.

ADJUSTABLE-RATE MORTGAGE (ARM): A mortgage in which the interest changes periodically, according to corresponding fluctuations in an index. All ARMs are tied to indexes.

ADJUSTMENT DATE: The date the interest rate changes on an adjustable-rate mortgage.

AMORTIZATION: The loan payment consists of a portion which will be applied to pay the accruing interest on a loan, with the remainder being applied to the principal. Over time, the interest portion decreases (as the loan balance decreases) and the portion of the loan payment applied to the principal increases so that the loan is paid off (amortized) in the specified time.

AMORTIZATION SCHEDULE: A table which shows how much of each payment will be applied toward principal and how much toward interest over the life of the loan. It also shows the gradual decrease of the loan balance until it reaches zero.

ANNUAL PERCENTAGE RATE (APR): This is not the note rate on your loan. It is a value created according to a government formula intended to reflect the true annual cost of borrowing, expressed as a percentage. It works sort of like this, but not exactly, so only uses this as a guideline: deduct the closing costs from your loan amount, then using your actual loan payment, calculate what the interest rate would be on this amount instead of your actual loan amount. You will come up with a number close to the APR. Because you are using the same payment on a smaller amount, the APR is always higher than the actual rate on your loan.

APPLICATION: The form used to apply for a mortgage loan, containing information about a borrower's income, savings, assets, debts, and more.

APPRAISAL: A written justification of the price paid for a property, primarily based on an analysis of comparable sales of similar homes nearby.

APPRAISED VALUE: An opinion of a property's fair market value, based on an appraiser's knowledge, experience, and analysis of the property. Since an appraisal is based primarily on comparable sales, and the most recent sale is the one on the property in question, the appraisal usually comes out at the purchase price.

APPRAISER: An individual qualified by education, training, and experience to estimate the value of real property and personal property. Although some appraisers work directly for mortgage lenders, most are independent.

APPRECIATION: The increase in the value of a property due to changes in market conditions, inflation, or other causes.

ASSESSED VALUE: The valuation placed on property by a public tax assessor for purposes of taxation.

ASSESSMENT: The placing of a value on property for the purpose of taxation.

ASSESSOR: A public official who establishes the value of a property for taxation purposes.

ASSET: Item of value owned by an individual. Assets that can be quickly converted into cash are considered "liquid assets." These include bank accounts, stocks, bonds, mutual funds, and so on. Other assets include real estate, personal property, and debts owed to an individual by others.

ASSIGNMENT: When ownership of your mortgage is transferred from one company or individual to another, it is called an assignment.

ASSUMABLE MORTGAGE: A mortgage that can be assumed by the buyer when a home is sold. Usually, the borrower must "qualify" in order to assume the loan.

ASSUMPTION: The term applied when a buyer assumes the seller's mortgage.

BALLOON MORTGAGE: A mortgage loan that requires the remaining principal balance be paid at a specific point in time. For example, a loan may be amortized as if it would be paid over a thirty year period, but requires that at the end of the tenth year the entire remaining balance must be paid.

BALLOON PAYMENT: The final lump sum payment that is due at the termination of a balloon mortgage.

BANKRUPTCY: By filing in federal bankruptcy court, an individual or individuals can restructure or relieve themselves of debts and liabilities. Bankruptcies are of various types, but the most common for an individual seem to be a "Chapter 7 No Asset" bankruptcy which relieves the borrower of most types of debt. A borrower cannot usually qualify for an "A" paper loan for a period of two years after the bankruptcy has been discharged and requires the re-establishment of an ability to repay debt.

BILL OF SALE: A written document that transfers title to personal property. For example, when selling an automobile to acquire funds which will be used as a source of down payment or for closing costs, the lender will usually require the bill of sale (in addition to other items) to help document this source of funds.

BIWEEKLY MORTGAGE: A mortgage in which you make payments every two weeks instead of once a month. The basic result is that instead of making twelve monthly payments during the year, you make the equivalent of thirteen. The extra payment reduces the principal, substantially reducing the time it takes to pay off a thirty year mortgage. *Note:* there are independent companies that encourage you to set up bi-weekly payment schedules with them on your thirty year mortgage. They charge a set-up fee and a transfer fee for every payment. Your funds are deposited into a trust account from which your monthly payment is then made, and the excess funds then remain in the trust account until enough has accrued to make the additional payment which will then be paid to reduce your principle. You could save money by doing the same thing yourself, plus you have to have faith that once you transfer money to them that they will actually transfer your funds to your lender.

BOND MARKET: Usually refers to the daily buying and selling of thirty year treasury bonds. Lenders follow this market intensely because as the yields of bonds go up and down, fixed rate mortgages do approximately the same thing. The same factors that affect the Treasury bond market also affect mortgage rates at the same time.

That is why rates change daily, and in a volatile market can and do change during the day as well.

BRIDGE LOAN: Not used much anymore, bridge loans are obtained by those who have not yet sold their previous property, but must close on a purchase property. The bridge loan becomes the source of their funds for the down payment. One reason for their fall from favor is that there are more and more second mortgage lenders now that will lend at a high loan to value ratio. In addition, sellers often prefer to accept offers from buyers who have already sold their property.

BROKER: Broker has several meanings in different situations. Most REALTORs® are "agents" who work under a "broker." Some agents are brokers as well, either working for themselves or under another broker. In the mortgage industry, broker usually refers to a company or individual that does not lend the money for the loans themselves, but broker loans to larger lenders or investors. As a normal definition, a broker is anyone who acts as an agent bringing two parties together for any type of transaction and earns a fee for doing so.

BUY DOWN: Usually refers to a fixed rate mortgage where the interest rate is "bought down" for a temporary period, usually one to three years. After that time and for the remainder of the term, the borrower's payment is calculated at the note rate. In order to buy down the initial rate for the temporary payment, a lump sum is paid and held in an account used to supplement the borrower's monthly payment. These funds usually come from the seller (or some other source) as a financial incentive to induce someone to buy their property. A "lender funded buy down" is when the lender pays the initial lump sum. They can accomplish this because the note rate on the loan (after the buy down adjustments) will be higher than the current market rate. One reason for doing this is because the borrower may get to "qualify" at the start rate for a higher loan amount. Another reason is that a borrower may expect his earnings to go up substantially in the near future, but wants a lower payment right now.

CALL OPTION: Similar to the "Acceleration Clause."

CAP: Adjustable Rate Mortgages have fluctuating interest rates, but those fluctuations are usually limited to a certain amount. Those limitations may apply to how much the loan may adjust over a six-month period, an annual period, and/or over the life of the loan. They are referred to as "caps." Some ARMs, although they may have a life cap, allow the interest rate to fluctuate freely, but require a certain minimum payment (which can change once a year). There is a limit on how much that payment can change each year, and that limit is also referred to as a cap.

CASH-OUT REFINANCE: When a borrower refinances his mortgage at a higher amount than the current loan balance with the intention of pulling out money for personal use, it is referred to as "cash out refinance."

CERTIFICATE OF DEPOSIT: A time deposit held in a bank that pays a certain amount of interest to the depositor.

CERTIFICATE OF DEPOSIT INDEX: One of the indexes used for determining interest rate changes on some adjustable rate mortgages. It is an average of what banks are paying on certificates of deposit.

CERTIFICATE OF ELIGIBILITY: A document issued by the Veterans Administration that certifies a veteran's eligibility for a VA loan.

CERTIFICATE OF REASONABLE VALUE (CRV): Once the appraisal has been performed on a property being bought with a VA loan, the Veterans Administration issues a CRV.

CHAIN OF TITLE: An analysis of the transfers of title to a piece of property over the years.

CLEAR TITLE: A title that is free of liens or legal questions as to ownership of the property.

CLOSING: This has different meanings in different states. In some states a real estate transaction is not consider "closed" until the documents record at the local recorders office. In others, the "closing" is a meeting where all of the documents are signed and money changes hands.

CLOSING COSTS: Closing costs are separated into what are called "non-recurring closing costs" and "pre-paid items." Non-recurring closing costs are any items that are paid just once as a result of buying the property or obtaining a loan. "Pre-paids" are items that recur over time, such as property taxes and homeowners insurance. A lender makes an attempt to estimate the amount of non-recurring closing costs and prepaid items on the Good Faith Estimate, which they must issue to the borrower within three days of receiving a home loan application.

CLOSING STATEMENT: See "HUD-1 Settlement Statement."

CLOUD ON TITLE: Any conditions revealed by a title search that adversely affects the title to real estate. Usually clouds on title cannot be removed except by deed, release, or court action.

CO-BORROWER: An additional individual who is both obligated on the loan and is on title to the property.

COLLATERAL: In a home loan, the property is the collateral. The borrower risks losing the property if the loan is not repaid according to the terms of the mortgage or deed of trust.

COLLECTION: When a borrower falls behind, the lender contacts them in an effort to bring the loan current. The loan goes to "collection." As part of the collection effort, the lender must mail and record certain documents in case they are eventually required to foreclose on the property.

COMMISSION: Most salespeople earn commissions for the work that they do. There are many sales professionals involved in each transaction, including REALTORs®, loan officers, title representatives, attorneys, escrow representative, and representatives for pest companies, home warranty companies, home inspection companies, insurance agents, and more. The commissions are paid out of the charges paid by the seller or buyer in the purchase transaction. REALTORs® generally earn the largest commissions, followed by lenders, then the others.

COMMON AREA ASSESSMENTS: In some areas they are called Homeowners Association Fees. They are charges paid to the Homeowners Association by the owners of the individual units in a condominium or planned unit development (PUD) and are generally used to maintain the property and common areas.

COMMON AREAS: Those portions of a building, land, and amenities owned (or managed) by a planned unit development (PUD) or condominium project's homeowners' association (or a cooperative project's cooperative corporation) that are used by all of the unit owners who share the common expenses of their operation and maintenance. Common areas include swimming pools, tennis courts, and other recreational facilities, as well as common corridors of buildings, parking areas, means of ingress and egress, etc.

COMMON LAW: An unwritten body of law based on general custom in England and is used to an extent in some states.

COMMUNITY PROPERTY: In some states, especially the southwest, property acquired by a married couple during their marriage is considered to be owned jointly (except under special circumstances). This is an outgrowth of the Spanish and Mexican heritage of the area.

COMPARABLE SALES: Recent sales of similar properties in nearby areas and used to help determine the market value of a property. Also referred to as "comps."

CONDOMINIUM: A type of ownership in real property where all of the owners own the property, common areas and buildings together, with the exception of the interior of the unit to which they have title. Often mistakenly referred to as a type of construction or development, it actually refers to the type of ownership.

CONDOMINIUM CONVERSION: Changing the ownership of an existing building (usually a rental project) to the condominium form of ownership.

CONDOMINIUM HOTEL: A condominium project that has rental or registration desks, short-term occupancy, food and telephone services, and daily cleaning services. It is operated as a commercial hotel even though the units are individually owned. These are often found in resort areas like Hawaii.

CONSTRUCTION LOAN: A short-term, interim loan for financing the cost of construction. The lender makes payments to the builder at periodic intervals as the work progresses.

CONTINGENCY: A condition that must be met before a contract is legally binding. For example, home purchasers often include a contingency that specifies that the contract is not binding until the purchaser obtains a satisfactory home inspection report from a qualified home inspector.

CONTRACT: An oral or written agreement to do or to not do a certain thing.

CONVENTIONAL MORTGAGE: Refers to home loans other than government loans (VA and FHA).

CONVERTIBLE ARM: An adjustable-rate mortgage that allows the borrower to change the ARM to a fixed-rate mortgage within a specified time.

COOPERATIVE (CO-OP): A type of multiple ownership in which the residents of a multiunit housing complex own shares in the cooperative corporation that owns the property, giving each resident the right to occupy a specific apartment or unit.

COST OF FUNDS INDEX (COFI): One of the indexes that are used to determine interest rate changes for certain adjustable-rate mortgages. It represents the weighted-average cost of savings, borrowings, and advances of the financial institutions such as banks and savings & loans, in the 11th District of the Federal Home Loan Bank.

CREDIT: An agreement in which a borrower receives something of value in exchange for a promise to repay the lender at a later date.

CREDIT HISTORY: A record of an individual's repayment of debt. Credit histories are reviewed by mortgage lenders as one of the underwriting criteria in determining credit risk.

CREDITOR: A person to whom money is owed.

CREDIT REPORT: A report of an individual's credit history prepared by a credit bureau and used by a lender in determining a loan applicant's creditworthiness.

CREDIT REPOSITORY: An organization that gathers, records, updates, and stores financial and public records information about the payment records of individuals who are being considered for credit.

DEBT: An amount owed to another.

DEED: The legal document conveying title to a property.

DEED-IN-LIEU: Short for "deed in lieu of foreclosure," this conveys title to the lender when the borrower is in default and wants to avoid foreclosure. The lender may or may not cease foreclosure activities if a borrower asks to provide a deed-in-lieu. Regardless of whether the lender accepts the deed-in-lieu, the avoidance and non-repayment of debt will most likely show on a credit history. What a deed-in-lieu may prevent is having the documents preparatory to a foreclosure being recorded and become a matter of public record.

DEED OF TRUST: Some states, like California, do not record mortgages. Instead, they record a deed of trust, which is essentially the same thing.

DEFAULT: Failure to make the mortgage payment within a specified period of time. For first mortgages or first trust deeds, if a payment has still not been made within 30 days of the due date, the loan is considered to be in default.

DELINQUENCY: Failure to make mortgage payments when mortgage payments are due. For most mortgages, payments are due on the first day of the month. Even though they may not charge a "late fee" for a number of days, the payment is still considered to be late and the loan delinquent. When a loan payment is more than 30 days late, most lenders report the late payment to one or more credit bureaus.

DEPOSIT: A sum of money given in advance of a larger amount being expected in the future. In real estate it is often called an "earnest money deposit."

DEPRECIATION: A decline in the value of property; the opposite of appreciation. Depreciation is also an accounting term that shows the declining monetary value of an asset and is used as an expense to reduce taxable income. Since this is not a true expense where money is actually paid, lenders will add back depreciation expenses for self-employed borrowers and count it as income.

DISCOUNT POINTS: In the mortgage industry, this term is usually only used in reference to government loans, meaning FHA and VA loans. Discount points refer to any "points" paid in addition to the one percent loan origination fee. A "point" is one percent of the loan amount.

DOWN PAYMENT: The part of the purchase price of a property that the buyer pays in cash and does not finance with a mortgage.

DUE-ON-SALE PROVISION: A provision in a mortgage that allows the lender to demand repayment in full if the borrower sells the property that serves as security for the mortgage.

EARNEST MONEY DEPOSIT: A deposit made by the potential homebuyer to show that he or she is serious about buying the house.

EASEMENT: A right of way giving persons other than the owner access to or over a property.

EFFECTIVE AGE: An appraiser's estimate of the physical condition of a building. The actual age of a building may be shorter or longer than its effective age.

EMINENT DOMAIN: The right of a government to take private property for public use upon payment of its fair market value. Eminent domain is the basis for condemnation proceedings.

ENCROACHMENT: An improvement that intrudes illegally on another's property.

ENCUMBRANCE: Anything that affects or limits the fee simple title to a property, such as mortgages, leases, easements, or restrictions.

EQUAL CREDIT OPPORTUNITY ACT (ECOA): A federal law that requires lenders and other creditors to make credit equally available without discrimination based on race, color, religion, national origin, age, sex, marital status, or receipt of income from public assistance programs.

EQUITY: A homeowner's financial interest in a property. Equity is the difference between the fair market value of the property and the amount still owed on its mortgage and other liens.

ESCROW: An item of value, money, or documents deposited with a third party to be delivered upon the fulfillment of a condition. For example, the earnest money deposit is put into escrow until delivered to the seller when the transaction is closed.

ESCROW ACCOUNT: Once you close your purchase transaction, you may have an escrow account or impound account with your lender. This means the amount you pay each month includes an amount above what would be required if you were only paying your principal and interest. The extra money is held in your impound account (escrow account) for the payment of items like property taxes and homeowner's insurance when they come due. The lender pays them with your money instead of you paying them yourself.

ESCROW ANALYSIS: Once each year your lender will perform an "escrow analysis" to make sure they are collecting the correct amount of money for the anticipated expenditures.

ESCROW DISBURSEMENTS: The use of escrow funds to pay real estate taxes, hazard insurance, mortgage insurance, and other property expenses as they become due.

ESTATE: The ownership interest of an individual in real property. It is the sum total of all the real property and personal property owned by an individual at the time of their death.

EVICTION: The lawful expulsion of an occupant from real property.

EXAMINATION OF TITLE: The report on the title of a property from the public records or an abstract of the title.

EXCLUSIVE LISTING: A written contract that gives a licensed real estate agent the exclusive right to sell a property for a specified time.

EXECUTOR: A person named in a will to administer an estate. The court will appoint an administrator if no executor is named. "Executrix" is the feminine form.

FAIR CREDIT REPORTING ACT: A consumer protection law that regulates the disclosure of consumer credit reports by consumer/credit reporting agencies and establishes procedures for correcting mistakes on one's credit record.

FAIR MARKET VALUE: The highest price that a buyer, willing but not compelled to buy, would pay, and the lowest price a seller, willing but not compelled to sell, would accept.

FANNIE MAE (FNMA): The Federal National Mortgage Association, which is a congressionally chartered, shareholder-owned company that is the nation's largest supplier of home mortgage funds.

FANNIE MAE'S COMMUNITY HOME BUYER'S PROGRAM: An income-based community lending model, under which mortgage insurers and Fannie Mae offer flexible underwriting guidelines to increase a low- or moderate-income family's buying power and to decrease the total amount of cash needed to purchase a home. Borrowers who participate in this model are required to attend pre-purchase home-buyer education sessions.

FEDERAL HOUSING ADMINISTRATION (FHA): An agency of the U.S. Department of Housing and Urban Development (HUD). Its main activity is the insuring of residential mortgage loans made by private lenders. The FHA sets standards for construction and underwriting but does not lend money or plan or construct housing.

FEE SIMPLE: The greatest possible interest a person can have in real estate.

FEE SIMPLE ESTATE: An unconditional, unlimited estate of inheritance that represents the greatest estate and most extensive interest in land that can be enjoyed. It is of perpetual duration. When the real estate is in a condominium project, the unit owner is the exclusive owner only of the air space within his or her portion of the building (the unit) and is an owner in common with respect to the land and other common portions of the property.

FHA MORTGAGES: A mortgage that is insured by the Federal Housing Administration (FHA). Along with VA loans, an FHA loan will often be referred to as a government loan.

FIRM COMMITMENT: A lender's agreement to make a loan to a specific borrower on a specific property.

FIRST MORTGAGE: The mortgage that is in first place among any loans recorded against a property. Usually refers to the date in which loans are recorded, but there are exceptions.

FIXED-RATE MORTGAGE: A mortgage in which the interest rate does not change during the entire term of the loan.

FIXTURE: Personal property that becomes real property when attached in a permanent manner to real estate.

FLOOD INSURANCE: Insurance that compensates for physical property damage resulting from flooding. It is required for properties located in federally designated flood areas.

FORECLOSURE: The legal process by which a borrower in default under a mortgage is deprived of his or her interest in the mortgaged property. This usually involves a forced sale of the property at public auction with the proceeds of the sale being applied to the mortgage debt.

GOVERNMENT LOAN (MORTGAGE): A mortgage that is insured by the Federal Housing Administration (FHA) or guaranteed by the Department of Veterans Affairs (VA) or the Rural Housing Service (RHS). Mortgages that are not government loans are classified as conventional loans.

GOVERNMENT NATIONAL MORTGAGE ASSOCIATION (GINNIE MAE): A government-owned corporation within the U.S. Department of Housing and Urban Development (HUD). Created by Congress on September 1, 1968, GNMA performs the same role as Fannie Mae and Freddie Mac in providing funds to lenders for making home loans. The difference is that Ginnie Mae provides funds for government loans (FHA and VA)

GRANTEE: The person to whom an interest in real property is conveyed.

GRANTOR: The person conveying an interest in real property.

HAZARD INSURANCE: Insurance coverage for physical damage to a property from fire, wind, vandalism, or other hazards.

HOME EQUITY CONVERSION MORTGAGE (HECM): Usually referred to as a reverse annuity mortgage, what makes this type of mortgage unique is that instead of making payments to a lender, the lender makes payments to you. It enables older home owners to convert the equity they have in their homes into cash, usually in the form of monthly payments. Unlike traditional home equity loans, a borrower does not qualify on the basis of income but on the value of his or her home. In addition, the loan does not have to be repaid until the borrower no longer occupies the property.

HOME EQUITY LINE OF CREDIT: A mortgage loan, usually in second position, that allows the borrower to obtain cash drawn against the equity of his home, up to a predetermined amount.

HOME INSPECTION: A thorough inspection by a professional that evaluates the structural and mechanical condition of a property. A satisfactory home inspection is often included as a contingency by the purchaser.

HOMEOWNERS' ASSOCIATION: A nonprofit association that manages the common areas of a planned unit development (PUD) or condominium project. In a condominium project, it has no ownership interest in the common elements. In a PUD project, it holds title to the common elements.

HOMEOWNER'S INSURANCE: An insurance policy that combines personal liability insurance and hazard insurance coverage for a dwelling and its contents.

HOMEOWNER'S WARRANTY: A type of insurance often purchased by homebuyers that will cover repairs to certain items, such as heating or air conditioning, should they break down within the coverage period. The buyer often requests the seller to pay for this coverage as a condition of the sale, but either party can pay.

HUD MEDIAN INCOME: Median family income for a particular county or metropolitan statistical area (MSA), as estimated by the Department of Housing and Urban Development (HUD).

HUD-1 SETTLEMENT STATEMENT: A document that provides an itemized listing of the funds that were paid at closing. Items that appear on the statement include real estate commissions, loan fees, points, and initial escrow (impound) amounts. Each type of expense goes on a specific numbered line on the sheet. The totals at the bottom of the HUD-1 statement define the seller's net proceeds and the buyer's net payment at closing. It is called a HUD-1 because the form is printed by the Department of Housing and Urban Development (HUD). The HUD-1 statement is also known as the "closing statement" or "settlement sheet."

JOINT TENANCY: A form of ownership or taking title to property which means each party owns the whole property and that ownership is not separate. In the event of the death of one party, the survivor owns the property in its entirety.

JUDGMENT: A decision made by a court of law. In judgments that require the repayment of a debt, the court may place a lien against the debtor's real property as collateral for the judgment's creditor.

JUDICIAL FORECLOSURE: A type of foreclosure proceeding used in some states that is handled as a civil lawsuit and conducted entirely under the auspices of a court. Other states use non-judicial foreclosure.

JUMBO LOAN: A loan that exceeds Fannie Mae's and Freddie Mac's loan limits, currently at $227,150. It is also called a nonconforming loan. Freddie Mac and Fannie Mae loans are referred to as conforming loans.

LATE CHARGE: The penalty a borrower must pay when a payment is made a stated number of days late. On a first trust deed or mortgage, this is usually fifteen days.

LEASE: A written agreement between the property owner and a tenant that stipulates the payment and conditions under which the tenant may possess the real estate for a specified period of time.

LEASEHOLD ESTATE: A way of holding title to a property wherein the mortgager does not actually own the property but rather has a recorded long-term lease on it.

LEASE OPTION: An alternative financing option that allows homebuyers to lease a home with an option to buy. Each month's rent payment may consist of not only the rent, but an additional amount which can be applied toward the down payment on an already specified price.

LEGAL DESCRIPTION: A property description, recognized by law, that is sufficient to locate and identify the property without oral testimony.

LENDER: A term which can refer to the institution making the loan or to the individual representing the firm. For example, loan officers are often referred to as "lenders."

LIABILITIES: A person's financial obligations. Liabilities include long-term and short-term debt, as well as any other amounts that are owed to others.

LIABILITY INSURANCE: Insurance coverage that offers protection against claims alleging that a property owner's negligence or inappropriate action resulted in bodily injury or property damage to another party. It is usually part of a homeowner's insurance policy.

LIEN: A legal claim against a property that must be paid off when the property is sold. A mortgage or first trust deed is considered a lien.

LIFE CAP: For an adjustable-rate mortgage (ARM), a limit on the amount that the interest rate can increase or decrease over the life of the mortgage.

LINE OF CREDIT: An agreement by a commercial bank or other financial institution to extend credit up to a certain amount for a certain time to a specified borrower.

LIQUID ASSET: A cash asset or an asset that is easily converted into cash.

LOAN: A sum of borrowed money (principal) that is generally repaid with interest.

LOAN OFFICER: Also referred to by a variety of other terms, such as lender, loan representative, loan "rep," account executive, and others. The loan officer serves several functions and has various responsibilities: they solicit loans, they are the representative of the lending institution, and they represent the borrower to the lending institution.

LOAN ORIGINATION: How a lender refers to the process of obtaining new loans.

LOAN SERVICING: After you obtain a loan, the company you make the payments to is "servicing" your loan. They process payments, send statements, manage the escrow/impound account, provide collection efforts on delinquent loans, ensure that insurance and property taxes are made on the property, handle pay-offs and assumptions, and provide a variety of other services.

LOAN-TO-VALUE (LTV): The percentage relationship between the amounts of the loan and the appraised value or sales price (whichever is lower).

LOCK-IN: An agreement in which the lender guarantees a specified interest rate for a certain amount of time at a certain cost.

LOCK-IN PERIOD: The time period during which the lender has guaranteed an interest rate for a certain amount of time at a certain cost.

MARGIN: The difference between the interest rate and the index on an adjustable rate mortgage. The margin remains stable over the life of the loan. It is the index which moves up and down.

MATURITY: The date on which the principal balance of a loan, bond, or other financial instrument becomes due and payable.

MERGED CREDIT REPORT: A credit report which reports the

raw data pulled from two or more of the major credit repositories. Contrast with a Residential Mortgage Credit Report (RMCR) or a standard factual credit report.

MODIFICATION: Occasionally, a lender will agree to modify the terms of your mortgage without requiring you to refinance. If any changes are made, it is called a modification.

MORTGAGE: A legal document that pledges a property to the lender as security for payment of a debt. Instead of mortgages, some states use First Trust Deeds.

MORTGAGE BANKER: A mortgage banker is generally assumed to originate and fund their own loans, which are then sold on the secondary market, usually to Fannie Mae, Freddie Mac, or Ginnie Mae. However, firms rather loosely apply this term to themselves, whether they are true mortgage bankers or simply mortgage brokers or correspondents.

MORTGAGE BROKER: A mortgage company that originates loans, then places those loans with a variety of other lending institutions with which they usually have pre-established relationships.

MORTGAGEE: The lender in a mortgage agreement.

MORTGAGE INSURANCE (MI): Insurance that covers the lender against some of the losses incurred as a result of a default on a home loan. Often mistakenly referred to as PMI, which is actually the name of one of the larger mortgage insurers. Mortgage insurance is usually required in one form or another on all loans that have a loan-to-value ratio higher than eighty percent. Mortgages above 80% LTV that call themselves "No MI" are usually made at a higher interest rate. Instead of the borrower paying the mortgage insurance premiums directly, they pay a higher interest rate to the lender, which then pays the mortgage insurance themselves. Also, FHA loans and certain first-time homebuyer programs require mortgage insurance regardless of the loan-to-value.

MORTGAGE INSURANCE PREMIUM (MIP): The amount paid by a mortgagor for mortgage insurance, either to a government agency such as the Federal Housing Administration (FHA) or to a private mortgage insurance (MI) company.

MORTGAGE LIFE AND DISABILITY INSURANCE: A type of term life insurance often bought by borrowers. The amount of coverage decreases as the principal balance declines. Some policies also cover the borrower in the event of disability. In the event that the borrower dies while the policy is in force, the debt is automatically satisfied by insurance proceeds. In the case of disability insurance, the insurance will make the mortgage payment for a specified amount of time during the disability. Be careful to read the terms of coverage, however, because often the coverage does not start immediately upon the disability, but after a specified period, sometimes forty-five days.

MORTGAGOR: The borrower in a mortgage agreement.

MULTI DWELLING UNITS: Properties that provide separate housing units for more than one family, although they secure only a single mortgage.

NEGATIVE AMORTIZATION: Some adjustable rate mortgages allow the interest rate to fluctuate independently of a required minimum payment. If a borrower makes the minimum payment it may not cover all of the interest that would normally be due at the current interest rate. In essence, the borrower is deferring the interest payment, which is why this is called "deferred interest." The deferred interest is added to the balance of the loan and the loan balance grows larger instead of smaller, which is called negative amortization.

NO CASH-OUT REFINANCE: A refinance transaction that is not intended to put cash in the hand of the borrower. Instead, the new balance is calculated to cover the balance due on the current loan and any costs associated with obtaining the new mortgage. It is often referred to as a "rate and term refinance."

NO-COST LOAN: Many lenders offer loans that you can obtain at "no cost." You should inquire whether this means there are no "lender" costs associated with the loan, or if it also covers the other costs you would normally have in a purchase or refinance transaction, such as title insurance, escrow fees, settlement fees, appraisal, recording fees, notary fees, and others. These are fees and costs that may be associated with buying a home or obtaining a loan, but not charged directly by the lender. Keep in mind that like a "no-point" loan, the interest rate will be higher than if you obtain a loan that has costs associated with it.

NO-POINT LOAN: Almost all lenders offer loans at "no points." You will find the interest rate on a "no points" loan is approximately a quarter percent higher than on a loan where you pay one point.

NOTE: A legal document that obligates a borrower to repay a mortgage loan at a stated interest rate during a specified period of time.

NOTE RATE: The interest rate stated on a mortgage note.

NOTICE OF DEFAULT: A formal written notice to a borrower that a default has occurred and that legal action may be taken.

ORIGINAL PRINCIPAL BALANCE: The total amount of principal owed on a mortgage before any payments are made.

ORIGINATION FEE: On a government loan the loan origination fee is one percent of the loan amount, but additional points may be charged which are called "discount points." One point equals one percent of the loan amount. On a conventional loan, the loan origination fee refers to the total number of points a borrower pays.

OWNER FINANCING: A property purchase transaction in which the property seller provides all or part of the financing.

PARTIAL PAYMENT: A payment that is not sufficient to cover the scheduled monthly payment on a mortgage loan. Normally, a lender will not accept a partial payment, but in times of hardship you can make this request of the loan servicing collection department.

PAYMENT CHANGE DATE: The date when a new monthly payment amount takes effect on an adjustable-rate mortgage (ARM) or a graduated-payment mortgage (GPM). Generally, the payment change date occurs in the month immediately after the interest rate adjustment date.

PERIODIC PAYMENT CAP For an adjustable-rate mortgage where the interest rate and the minimum payment amount fluctuate independently of one another, this is a limit on the amount that payments can increase or decrease during any one-adjustment period.

PERIODIC RATE CAP: For an adjustable-rate mortgage, a limit on the amount that the interest rate can increase or decrease during any one-adjustment period, regardless of how high or low the index might be.

PERSONAL PROPERTY: Any property that is not real property.

PITI: This stands for principal, interest, taxes and insurance. If you have an "impounded" loan, then your monthly payment to the lender includes all of these and probably includes mortgage insurance as well. If you do not have an impounded account, then the lender still calculates this amount and uses it as part of determining your debt-to-income ratio.

PITI RESERVES: A cash amount that a borrower must have on hand after making a down payment and paying all closing costs for the purchase of a home. The principal, interest, taxes, and insurance

(PITI) reserves must equal the amount that the borrower would have to pay for PITI for a predefined number of months.

PLANNED UNIT DEVELOPMENT (PUD): A type of ownership where individuals actually own the building or unit they live in, but common areas are owned jointly with the other members of the development or association. Contrast with condominium, where an individual actually owns the airspace of his unit, but the buildings and common areas are owned jointly with the others in the development or association.

POINT: A point is 1 percent of the amount of the mortgage.

POWER OF ATTORNEY: A legal document that authorizes another person to act on one's behalf. A power of attorney can grant complete authority or can be limited to certain acts and/or certain periods of time.

PRE-APPROVAL: A loosely used term which is generally taken to mean that a borrower has completed a loan application and provided debt, income, and savings documentation which an underwriter has reviewed and approved. A pre-approval is usually done at a certain loan amount and making assumptions about what the interest rate will actually be at the time the loan is actually made, as well as estimates for the amount that will be paid for property taxes, insurance and others. A pre-approval applies only to the borrower. Once a property is chosen, it must also meet the underwriting guidelines of the lender. Contrast with pre-qualification

PREPAYMENT: Any amount paid to reduce the principal balance of a loan before the due date. It is payment in full on a mortgage that may result from a sale of the property, the owner's decision to pay off the loan in full, or a foreclosure. In each case, prepayment means payment occurs before the loan has been fully amortized.

PREPAYMENT PENALTY: A fee that may be charged to a borrower who pays off a loan before it is due.

PRE-QUALIFICATION: This usually refers to the loan officer's written opinion of the ability of a borrower to qualify for a home loan, after the loan officer has made inquiries about debt, income, and savings. The information provided to the loan officer may have been presented verbally or in the form of documentation, and the loan officer may or may not have reviewed a credit report on the borrower.

PRIME RATE: The interest rate that banks charge to their preferred customers. Changes in the prime rate are widely publicized in the news media and are used as the indexes in some adjustable rate mortgages, especially home equity lines of credit. Changes in the prime rate do not directly affect other types of mortgages, but the same factors that influence the prime rate also affect the interest rates of mortgage loans.

PRINCIPAL: The amount borrowed or remaining unpaid. It is the part of the monthly payment that reduces the remaining balance of a mortgage.

PRINCIPAL BALANCE: The outstanding balance of principal on a mortgage. The principal balance does not include interest or any other charges. See "Remaining Balance."

PRINCIPAL, INTEREST, TAXES, AND INSURANCE (PITI): The four components of a monthly mortgage payment on impounded loans. Principal refers to the part of the monthly payment that reduces the remaining balance of the mortgage. Interest is the fee charged for borrowing money. Taxes and insurance refer to the amounts that are paid into an escrow account each month for property taxes and mortgage and hazard insurance.

PRIVATE MORTGAGE INSURANCE (MI): Mortgage insurance that is provided by a private mortgage insurance company to protect lenders against loss if a borrower defaults. Most lenders generally require MI for a loan with a loan-to-value (LTV) percentage in excess of 80 percent.

PROMISSORY NOTE: A written promise to repay a specified amount over a specified period of time.

PUBLIC AUCTION: A meeting in an announced public location to sell property to repay a mortgage that is in default.

PLANNED UNIT DEVELOPMENT (PUD): A project or subdivision that includes common property that is owned and maintained by a homeowners' association for the benefit and use of the individual PUD unit owners.

PURCHASE AGREEMENT: A written contract signed by the buyer and seller stating the terms and conditions under which a property will be sold.

PURCHASE MONEY TRANSACTION: The acquisition of property through the payment of money or its equivalent.

QUALIFYING RATIOS: Calculations that are used in determining whether a borrower can qualify for a mortgage. There are two ratios. The "top" or "front" ratio is a calculation of the borrower's monthly housing costs (principle, taxes, insurance, mortgage insurance, and homeowner's association fees) as a percentage of monthly income. The "back" or "bottom" ratio includes housing costs as will as all other monthly debt.

QUITCLAIM DEED: A deed that transfers without warranty whatever interest or title a grantor may have at the time the conveyance is made.

RATE LOCKS: A commitment issued by a lender to a borrower or other mortgage originator guaranteeing a specified interest rate for a specified period of time at a specific cost.

REAL ESTATE AGENT: A person licensed to negotiate and transact the sale of real estate.

REAL ESTATE SETTLEMENT PROCEDURES ACT (RESPA): A consumer protection law that requires lenders to give borrowers advance notice of closing costs.

REAL PROPERTY: Land and appurtenances, including anything of a permanent nature such as structures, trees, minerals, and the interest, benefits, and inherent rights thereof.

REALTOR®: A real estate agent, broker or an associate who holds active membership in a local real estate board that is affiliated with the National Association of REALTORs®.

RECORDER: The public official who keeps records of transactions that affect real property in the area. It is sometimes known as a "Registrar of Deeds" or "County Clerk."

RECORDING: The noting in the registrar's office of the details of a properly executed legal document, such as a deed, a mortgage note, a satisfaction of mortgage, or an extension of mortgage, thereby makes it a part of the public record.

REFINANCE TRANSACTION: The process of paying off one loan with the proceeds from a new loan using the same property as security.

REMAINING BALANCE: The amount of principal that has not yet been repaid. See "Principal Balance."

REMAINING TERM: The original amortization term minus the number of payments that have been applied.

RENT LOSS INSURANCE: Insurance that protects a landlord against loss of rent or rental value due to fire or other casualty that renders the leased premises unavailable for use and as a result of which the tenant is excused from paying rent.

REPAYMENT PLAN: An arrangement made to repay delinquent installments or advances.

REPLACEMENT RESERVE FUND: A fund set aside for replacement of common property in a condominium, PUD, or cooperative project - particularly that which has a short life expectancy, such as carpeting, furniture, etc.

REVOLVING DEBT: A credit arrangement, such as a credit card, that allows a customer to borrow against a pre-approved line of credit when purchasing goods and services. The borrower is billed for the amount that is actually borrowed plus any interest due.

RIGHT OF FIRST REFUSAL: A provision in an agreement that requires the owner of a property to give another party the first opportunity to purchase or lease the property before he or she offers it for sale or lease to others.

RIGHT OF INGRESS OR EGRESS: The right to enter or leave designated premises.

RIGHT OF SURVIVORSHIP: In joint tenancy, the right of survivors to acquire the interest of a deceased joint tenant.

SALE-LEASEBACK: A technique in which a seller deeds property to a buyer for a consideration, and the buyer simultaneously leases the property back to the seller.

SECOND MORTGAGE: A mortgage that has a lien position subordinate to the first mortgage.

SECONDARY MARKET: The buying and selling of existing mortgages, usually as part of a "pool" of mortgages.

SECURED LOAN: A loan that is backed by collateral.

SECURITY: The property that will be pledged as collateral for a loan.

SELLERS CARRY-BACK: An agreement in which the owner of a property provides financing, often in combination with an assumable mortgage.

SERVICER: An organization that collects principal and interest payments from borrowers and manages borrowers' escrow accounts. The servicer often services mortgages that have been purchased by an investor in the secondary mortgage market.

SERVICING: The collection of mortgage payments from borrowers and related responsibilities of a loan servicer.

SETTLEMENT STATEMENT: See "HUD-1 Settlement Statement."

SUBDIVISION: A housing development that is created by dividing a tract of land into individual lots for sale or lease.

SUBORDINATE FINANCING: Any mortgage or other lien that has a priority that is lower than that of the first mortgage.

SURVEY: A drawing or map showing the precise legal boundaries of a property, the location of improvements, easements, rights of way, encroachments, and other physical features.

SWEAT EQUITY: Contribution to the construction or rehabilitation of a property in the form of labor or services rather than cash.

TENANCY IN COMMON: As opposed to joint tenancy, when there are two or more individuals on title to a piece of property, this type of ownership does not pass ownership to the others in the event of death.

THIRD-PARTY ORIGINATION: A process by which a lender uses another party to completely or partially originate, process, underwrite, close, fund, or package the mortgages it plans to deliver to the secondary mortgage market.

TITLE: A legal document evidencing a person's right to or ownership of a property.

TITLE COMPANY: A company that specializes in examining and insuring titles to real estate.

TITLE INSURANCE: Insurance that protects the lender (lender's policy) or the buyer (owner's policy) against loss arising from disputes over ownership of a property.

TITLE SEARCH: A check of the title records to ensure that the seller is the legal owner of the property and that there are no liens or other claims outstanding.

TRANSFER OF OWNERSHIP: Any means by which the ownership of a property changes hands. Lenders consider all of the following situations to be a transfer of ownership: the purchase of a property "subject to" the mortgage, the assumption of the mortgage debt by the property purchaser, and any exchange of possession of the property under a land sales contract or any other land trust device.

TRANSFER TAX: State or local tax payable when title passes from one owner to another.

TREASURY INDEX: An index that is used to determine interest rate changes for certain adjustable-rate mortgage (ARM) plans. It is based on the results of auctions that the U.S. Treasury holds for its Treasury bills and securities or is derived from the U.S. Treasury's daily yield curve, which is based on the closing market bid yields on actively traded Treasury securities in the over-the-counter market.

TRUTH-IN-LENDING: A federal law that requires lenders to fully disclose, in writing, the terms and conditions of a mortgage, including the annual percentage rate (APR) and other charges.

TWO-STEP MORTGAGES: An adjustable-rate mortgage (ARM) that has one interest rate for the first five or seven years of its mortgage term and a different interest rate for the remainder of the amortization term.

TWO TO FOUR FAMILY PROPERTY: A property that consists of a structure that provides living space (dwelling units) for two to four families, although ownership of the structure is evidenced by a single deed.

TRUSTEE: A fiduciary that holds or controls property for the benefit of another.

VA MORTGAGES: A mortgage that is guaranteed by the Department of Veterans Affairs (VA).

VESTED: Having the right to use a portion of a fund such as an individual retirement fund. For example, individuals who are 100 percent vested can withdraw all of the funds that are set aside for them in a retirement fund. However, taxes may be due on any funds that are actually withdrawn.

VETERANS ADMINISTRATION (VA): An agency of the federal government that guarantees residential mortgages made to eligible veterans of the military services. The guarantee protects the lender against loss and thus encourages lenders to make mortgages to veterans.

APPENDIX

APPENDIX 1

Licensing of Mortgage Brokers

NRS 645B.020 Application for license; application for branch offices; requirements for issuance of license.

1. A person who wishes to be licensed as a mortgage broker must file a written application for a license with the Office of the Commissioner and pay the fee required pursuant to NRS 645B.050. An application for a license as a mortgage broker must:

(a) Be verified.

(b) State the name, residence address and business address of the applicant and the location of each principal office and branch office at which the mortgage broker will conduct business within this State.

(c) State the name under which the applicant will conduct business as a mortgage broker.

(d) List the name, residence address and business address of each person who will:

(1) If the applicant is not a natural person, have an interest in the mortgage broker as a principal, partner, officer, director or trustee, specifying the capacity and title of each such person.

(2) Be associated with or employed by the mortgage broker as a mortgage agent.

(e) Include a general business plan and a description of the policies and procedures that the mortgage broker and his mortgage agents will follow to arrange and service loans and to conduct business pursuant to this chapter.

(f) State the length of time the applicant has been engaged in the business of a broker.

(g) Include a financial statement of the applicant and, if applicable, satisfactory proof that the applicant will be able to maintain continuously the net worth required pursuant to NRS 645B.115.

(h) Include all information required to complete the application.

(i) Include any other information required pursuant to the regulations adopted by the Commissioner or an order of the Commissioner.

2. If a mortgage broker will conduct business at one or more branch offices within this State, the mortgage broker must apply for a license for each such branch office.

3. Except as otherwise provided in this chapter, the Commissioner shall issue a license to an applicant as a mortgage broker if:

(a) The application complies with the requirements of this chapter; and

(b) The applicant and each general partner, officer or director of the applicant, if the applicant is a partnership, corporation or unincorporated association:

(1) Has a good reputation for honesty, trustworthiness and integrity and displays competence to transact the business of a mortgage broker in a manner which safeguards the interests of the general public. The applicant must submit satisfactory proof of these qualifications to the Commissioner.

(2) Has not been convicted of, or entered a plea of nolo contendere to, a felony relating to the practice of mortgage brokers or any crime involving fraud, misrepresentation or moral turpitude.

(3) Has not made a false statement of material fact on his application.

(4) Has not had a license that was issued pursuant to the provisions of this chapter or chapter 645E of NRS suspended or revoked within the 10 years immediately preceding the date of his application.

(5) Has not had a license that was issued in any other state, district or territory of the United States or any foreign country suspended or

revoked within the 10 years immediately preceding the date of his application.

(6) Has not violated any provision of this chapter or chapter 645E of NRS, a regulation adopted pursuant thereto or an order of the Commissioner.

(Added to NRS by 1973, 1536; A 1981, 1786; 1983, 1701; 1985, 2186; 1987, 1877; 1989, 1763; 1993, 495; 1997, 2171; 1999, 3780; 2001, 2464; 2003, 2721; 2005, 2781, 2807, 2816)

NRS 645B.023 Payment of child support: Submission of certain information by applicant; grounds for denial of license; duty of Commissioner. [Effective until the date of the repeal of the federal law requiring each state to establish procedures for withholding, suspending and restricting the professional, occupational and recreational licenses for child support arrearages and for noncompliance with certain processes relating to paternity or child support proceedings.]

1. In addition to any other requirements set forth in this chapter:

(a) A natural person who applies for the issuance of a license as a mortgage broker shall include the social security number of the applicant in the application submitted to the Commissioner.

(b) A natural person who applies for the issuance or renewal of a license as a mortgage broker shall submit to the Commissioner the statement prescribed by the Division of Welfare and Supportive Services of the Department of Health and Human Services pursuant to NRS 425.520. The statement must be completed and signed by the applicant.

2. The Commissioner shall include the statement required pursuant to subsection 1 in:

(a) The application or any other forms that must be submitted for the issuance or renewal of the license; or

(b) A separate form prescribed by the Commissioner.

3. A license as a mortgage broker may not be issued or renewed by the Commissioner if the applicant is a natural person who:

(a) Fails to submit the statement required pursuant to subsection 1; or

(b) Indicates on the statement submitted pursuant to subsection 1 that he is subject to a court order for the support of a child and is not in compliance with the order or a plan approved by the district attorney or other public agency enforcing the order for the repayment of the amount owed pursuant to the order.

4. If an applicant indicates on the statement submitted pursuant to subsection 1 that he is subject to a court order for the support of a child and is not in compliance with the order or a plan approved by the district attorney or other public agency enforcing the order for the repayment of the amount owed pursuant to the order, the Commissioner shall advise the applicant to contact the district attorney or other public agency enforcing the order to determine the actions that the applicant may take to satisfy the arrearage.

(Added to NRS by 1997, 2170; A 1999, 3782; 2005, 2783, 2807, 2810)

NRS 645B.023 Payment of child support: Submission of certain information by applicant; grounds for denial of license; duty of Commissioner. [Effective on the date of the repeal of the federal law requiring each state to establish procedures for withholding, suspending and restricting the professional, occupational and recreational licenses for child support arrearages and for noncompliance with certain processes relating to paternity or child support proceedings and expires by limitation 2 years after that date.]

1. In addition to any other requirements set forth in this chapter, a natural person who applies for the issuance or renewal of a license

as a mortgage broker shall submit to the Commissioner the statement prescribed by the Division of Welfare and Supportive Services of the Department of Health and Human Services pursuant to NRS 425.520. The statement must be completed and signed by the applicant.

2. The Commissioner shall include the statement required pursuant to subsection 1 in:

(a) The application or any other forms that must be submitted for the issuance or renewal of the license; or

(b) A separate form prescribed by the Commissioner.

3. A license as a mortgage broker may not be issued or renewed by the Commissioner if the applicant is a natural person who:

(a) Fails to submit the statement required pursuant to subsection 1; or

(b) Indicates on the statement submitted pursuant to subsection 1 that he is subject to a court order for the support of a child and is not in compliance with the order or a plan approved by the district attorney or other public agency enforcing the order for the repayment of the amount owed pursuant to the order.

4. If an applicant indicates on the statement submitted pursuant to subsection 1 that he is subject to a court order for the support of a child and is not in compliance with the order or a plan approved by the district attorney or other public agency enforcing the order for the repayment of the amount owed pursuant to the order, the Commissioner shall advise the applicant to contact the district attorney or other public agency enforcing the order to determine the actions that the applicant may take to satisfy the arrearage.

(Added to NRS by 1997, 2170; A 1999, 3782; 2005, 2783, 2807, 2810, effective on the date of the repeal of the federal law requiring each state to establish procedures for withholding, suspending and restricting the professional, occupational and recreational licenses for child support arrearages and for noncompliance with certain processes relating to paternity or child support proceedings)

NRS 645B.0243 Grounds for denial of license: Employing or associating with certain persons who are ineligible to be mortgage agents. The Commissioner may refuse to issue a license to an applicant if the Commissioner has reasonable cause to believe that the applicant or any general partner, officer or director of the applicant has, after October 1, 1999, employed or proposed to employ a person as a mortgage agent or authorized or proposed to authorize a person to be associated with a mortgage broker as a mortgage agent at a time when the applicant or the general partner, officer or director knew or, in light of all the surrounding facts and circumstances, reasonably should have known that the person:

1. Had been convicted of, or entered a plea of nolo contendere to:

(a) A felony relating to the practice of mortgage agents; or

(b) Any crime involving fraud, misrepresentation or moral turpitude; or

2. Had a financial services license or registration suspended or revoked within the immediately preceding 10 years.

(Added to NRS by 1999, 3768; A 2003, 2723)

NRS 645B.0245 Grounds for denial of license: Control by relative who would be ineligible to be licensed; act or omission of partner, officer or director.

1. If an applicant is a natural person, the Commissioner may refuse to issue a license to the applicant if the Commissioner has reasonable cause to believe that the applicant would be subject to control by a relative who would be ineligible to be licensed pursuant to this chapter.

2. If an applicant is a partnership, corporation or unincorporated association, the Commissioner may refuse to issue a license to the applicant if:

(a) Any member of the partnership or any officer or director of the corporation or unincorporated association has committed any act or omission that would be cause for refusing to issue a license to a natural person; or

(b) The Commissioner has reasonable cause to believe that any member of the partnership or any officer or director of the corporation or unincorporated association would be subject to control by a relative who would be ineligible to be licensed pursuant to this chapter.

(Added to NRS by 1999, 3769)

NRS 645B.0247 Grounds for denial of license: Authority of Commissioner not limited. The provisions of NRS 645B.0243 and 645B.0245 do not limit the authority of the Commissioner to refuse to issue a license to an applicant for any other lawful reason or pursuant to any other provision of law.

(Added to NRS by 1999, 3769)

NRS 645B.025 Posting of license; restrictions on transfer or assignment of license.

1. A mortgage broker shall post each license in a conspicuous place in the office to which it pertains.

2. A mortgage broker may not transfer or assign a license to another person, unless the Commissioner gives his written approval.

(Added to NRS by 1983, 1376; A 1983, 1843; 1987, 1877; 1999, 3782)

NRS 645B.035 Activities authorized by license; dual licensure as mortgage banker and mortgage broker.

1. A license as a mortgage broker entitles a licensee to engage only in the activities authorized by this chapter.

2. The provisions of this chapter do not prohibit a licensee from:

(a) Holding a license as a mortgage banker pursuant to chapter 645E of NRS; or

(b) Conducting the business of a mortgage banker and the business of a mortgage broker in the same office or place of business.

(Added to NRS by 1999, 3770; A 2003, 3548)

EXPIRATION AND RENEWAL OF BROKER'S LICENSE OR CERTIFICATE OF EXEMPTION; FEES

NRS 645B.050 Annual expiration of license or certificate of exemption; procedure for renewal; fees.

1. A license as a mortgage broker issued pursuant to this chapter expires each year on June 30, unless it is renewed. To renew such a license, the licensee must submit to the Commissioner on or before May 31 of each year:

(a) An application for renewal;

(b) The fee required to renew the license pursuant to this section;

(c) The information required pursuant to NRS 645B.051; and

(d) All information required to complete the renewal.

2. If the licensee fails to submit any item required pursuant to subsection 1 to the Commissioner on or before May 31 of any year, the license is cancelled as of June 30 of that year. The Commissioner may reinstate a cancelled license if the licensee submits to the Commissioner:

(a) An application for renewal;

(b) The fee required to renew the license pursuant to this section;

(c) The information required pursuant to NRS 645B.051;

(d) Except as otherwise provided in this section, a reinstatement fee of $200; and

(e) All information required to complete the reinstatement.

3. Except as otherwise provided in NRS 645B.016, a certificate of exemption issued pursuant to this chapter expires each year on December 31, unless it is renewed. To renew a certificate of exemption, a person must submit to the Commissioner on or before November 30 of each year:

(a) An application for renewal that includes satisfactory proof that the person meets the requirements for an exemption from the provisions of this chapter; and

(b) The fee required to renew the certificate of exemption.

4. If the person fails to submit any item required pursuant to subsection 3 to the Commissioner on or before November 30 of any year, the certificate of exemption is cancelled as of December 31 of that year. Except as otherwise provided in NRS 645B.016, the Commissioner may reinstate a cancelled certificate of exemption if the person submits to the Commissioner:

(a) An application for renewal that includes satisfactory proof that the person meets the requirements for an exemption from the provisions of this chapter;

(b) The fee required to renew the certificate of exemption; and

(c) Except as otherwise provided in this section, a reinstatement fee of $100.

5. Except as otherwise provided in this section, a person must pay the following fees to apply for, to be issued or to renew a license as a mortgage broker pursuant to this chapter:

(a) To file an original application for a license, $1,500 for the principal office and $40 for each branch office. The person must also pay such additional expenses incurred in the process of investigation as the Commissioner deems necessary.

(b) To be issued a license, $1,000 for the principal office and $60 for each branch office.

(c) To renew a license, $500 for the principal office and $100 for each branch office.

6. Except as otherwise provided in this section, a person must pay the following fees to apply for or to renew a certificate of exemption pursuant to this chapter:

(a) To file an application for a certificate of exemption, $200.

(b) To renew a certificate of exemption, $100.

7. To be issued a duplicate copy of any license or certificate of exemption, a person must make a satisfactory showing of its loss and pay a fee of $10.

8. Except as otherwise provided in this chapter, all fees received pursuant to this chapter must be deposited in the Fund for Mortgage Lending created by NRS 645F.270.

9. The Commissioner may, by regulation, increase any fee set forth in this section if the Commissioner determines that such an increase is necessary for the Commissioner to carry out his duties pursuant to this chapter. The amount of any increase in a fee pursuant to this subsection must not exceed the amount determined to be necessary for the Commissioner to carry out his duties pursuant to this chapter.

(Added to NRS by 1973, 1538; A 1975, 814; 1977, 1636; 1979, 120, 1094; 1981, 1788; 1983, 1320, 1379, 1702; 1985, 2187; 1987, 86, 1878; 1989, 1764; 1991, 177, 1803, 1825; 1993, 496; 1997, 2172; 1999, 3782; 2001, 2465; 2003, 3229, 3548; 2003, 20th Special Session, 265; 2005, 2784, 2807, 2817)

NRS 645B.051 Continuing education required for renewal of license.

1. Except as otherwise provided in this section, in addition to the requirements set forth in NRS 645B.050, to renew a license as a mortgage broker:

(a) If the licensee is a natural person, the licensee must submit to the Commissioner satisfactory proof that the licensee attended at least 10 hours of certified courses of continuing education during the 12 months immediately preceding the date on which the license expires.

(b) If the licensee is not a natural person, the licensee must submit to the Commissioner satisfactory proof that each natural person who supervises the daily business of the licensee attended at least 10 hours of certified courses of continuing education during the 12 months immediately preceding the date on which the license expires.

2. The Commissioner may provide by regulation that any hours of a certified course of continuing education attended during a 12-month period, but not needed to satisfy a requirement set forth in this section for the 12-month period in which the course was taken, may be used to satisfy a requirement set forth in this section for a later 12-month period.

3. As used in this section, "certified course of continuing education" means a course of continuing education which relates to the mortgage industry or mortgage transactions and which is certified by:

(a) The National Association of Mortgage Brokers or any successor in interest to that organization; or

(b) Any organization designated for this purpose by the Commissioner by regulation.

(Added to NRS by 2001, 2464; A 2003, 3551)

APPENDIX 2

REALTOR® Code of Ethics

As stated at The Association of REALTORS® Web Site (www.realtor. org/)

Code of Ethics and Standards of Practice
of the NATIONAL ASSOCIATION OF REALTORS®
Effective January 1, 2006

Where the word REALTORS® is used in this Code and Preamble, it shall be deemed to include REALTOR-ASSOCIATE®s.

While the Code of Ethics establishes obligations that may be higher than those mandated by law, in any instance where the Code of Ethics and the law conflict, the obligations of the law must take precedence.

Preamble

Under all is the land. Upon its wise utilization and widely allocated ownership depend the survival and growth of free institutions and of our civilization. REALTORS® should recognize that the interests of the nation and its citizens require the highest and best use of the land and the widest distribution of land ownership. They require the creation of adequate housing, the building of functioning cities, the development of productive industries and farms, and the preservation of a healthful environment.

Such interests impose obligations beyond those of ordinary commerce. They impose grave social responsibility and a patriotic duty to which

REALTORS® should dedicate themselves, and for which they should be diligent in preparing themselves. REALTORS®, therefore, are zealous to maintain and improve the standards of their calling and share with their fellow REALTORS® a common responsibility for its integrity and honor.

In recognition and appreciation of their obligations to clients, customers, the public, and each other, REALTORS® continuously strive to become and remain informed on issues affecting real estate and, as knowledgeable professionals, they willingly share the fruit of their experience and study with others. They identify and take steps, through enforcement of this Code of Ethics and by assisting appropriate regulatory bodies, to eliminate practices which may damage the public or which might discredit or bring dishonor to the real estate profession. REALTORS® having direct personal knowledge of conduct that may violate the Code of Ethics involving misappropriation of client or customer funds or property, willful discrimination, or fraud resulting in substantial economic harm, bring such matters to the attention of the appropriate Board or Association of REALTORS®. (Amended 1/00)

Realizing that cooperation with other real estate professionals promotes the best interests of those who utilize their services, REALTORS® urge exclusive representation of clients; do not attempt to gain any unfair advantage over their competitors; and they refrain from making unsolicited comments about other practitioners. In instances where their opinion is sought, or where REALTORS® believe that comment is necessary, their opinion is offered in an objective, professional manner, uninfluenced by any personal motivation or potential advantage or gain.

The term REALTOR® has come to connote competency, fairness, and high integrity resulting from adherence to a lofty ideal of moral conduct in business relations. No inducement of profit and no instruction from clients ever can justify departure from this ideal.

In the interpretation of this obligation, REALTORS® can take no safer guide than that which has been handed down through the centuries, embodied in the Golden Rule, "Whatsoever ye would that others should do to you, do ye even so to them."

Accepting this standard as their own, REALTORS® pledge to observe its spirit in all of their activities and to conduct their business in accordance with the tenets set forth below.

Duties to Clients and Customers

Article 1
When representing a buyer, seller, landlord, tenant, or other client as an agent, REALTORS® pledge themselves to protect and promote the interests of their client. This obligation to the client is primary, but it does not relieve REALTORS® of their obligation to treat all parties honestly. When serving a buyer, seller, landlord, tenant or other party in a non-agency capacity, REALTORS® remain obligated to treat all parties honestly. (Amended 1/01)

• Standard of Practice 1-1
REALTORS®, when acting as principals in a real estate transaction, remain obligated by the duties imposed by the Code of Ethics. (Amended 1/93)

• Standard of Practice 1-2
The duties the Code of Ethics imposes are applicable whether REALTORS® are acting as agents or in legally recognized non-agency

capacities except that any duty imposed exclusively on agents by law or regulation shall not be imposed by this Code of Ethics on REALTORS® acting in non-agency capacities.

As used in this Code of Ethics, "client" means the person(s) or entity(ies) with whom a REALTOR® or a REALTOR®'s firm has an agency or legally recognized non-agency relationship; "customer" means a party to a real estate transaction who receives information, services, or benefits but has no contractual relationship with the REALTOR® or the REALTOR®'s firm; "prospect" means a purchaser, seller, tenant, or landlord who is not subject to a representation relationship with the REALTOR® or REALTOR®'s firm; "agent" means a real estate licensee (including brokers and sales ASSOCIATES) acting in an agency relationship as defined by state law or regulation; and "broker" means a real estate licensee (including brokers and sales ASSOCIATES) acting as an agent or in a legally recognized non-agency capacity. (Adopted 1/95, Amended 1/04)

• Standard of Practice 1-3
REALTORS®, in attempting to secure a listing, shall not deliberately mislead the owner as to market value.

• Standard of Practice 1-4
REALTORS®, when seeking to become a buyer/tenant representative, shall not mislead buyers or tenants as to savings or other benefits that might be realized through use of the REALTOR®'s services. (Amended 1/93)

• Standard of Practice 1-5
REALTORS® may represent the seller/landlord and buyer/tenant in the same transaction only after full disclosure to and with informed consent of both parties. (Adopted 1/93)

• Standard of Practice 1-6
REALTORS® shall submit offers and counter-offers objectively and as quickly as possible. (Adopted 1/93, Amended 1/95)

• Standard of Practice 1-7
When acting as listing brokers, REALTORS® shall continue to submit to the seller/landlord all offers and counter-offers until closing or execution of a lease unless the seller/landlord has waived this obligation in writing. REALTORS® shall not be obligated to continue to market the property after an offer has been accepted by the seller/ landlord. REALTORS® shall recommend that sellers/ landlords obtain the advice of legal counsel prior to acceptance of a subsequent offer except where the acceptance is contingent on the termination of the pre-existing purchase contract or lease. (Amended 1/93)

• Standard of Practice 1-8
REALTORS®, acting as agents or brokers of buyers/tenants, shall submit to buyers/tenants all offers and counter-offers until acceptance but have no obligation to continue to show properties to their clients after an offer has been accepted unless otherwise agreed in writing. REALTORS®, acting as agents or brokers of buyers/tenants, shall recommend that buyers/tenants obtain the advice of legal counsel if there is a question as to whether a pre-existing contract has been terminated. (Adopted 1/93, Amended 1/99)

• Standard of Practice 1-9
The obligation of REALTORS® to preserve confidential information (as defined by state law) provided by their clients in the course of any agency relationship or non-agency relationship recognized by law continues after termination of agency relationships or any non-agency relationships recognized by law. REALTORS® shall not knowingly, during or following the termination of professional relationships with

their clients:

1) reveal confidential information of clients; or

2) use confidential information of clients to the disadvantage of clients; or

3) use confidential information of clients for the REALTOR®'s advantage or the advantage of third parties unless:

a) clients consent after full disclosure; or

b) REALTORS® are required by court order; or

c) it is the intention of a client to commit a crime and the information is necessary to prevent the crime; or

d) it is necessary to defend a REALTOR® or the REALTOR®'s employees or ASSOCIATES against an accusation of wrongful conduct.

Information concerning latent material defects is not considered confidential information under this Code of Ethics. (Adopted 1/93, Amended 1/01)

• Standard of Practice 1-10

REALTORS® shall, consistent with the terms and conditions of their real estate licensure and their property management agreement, competently manage the property of clients with due regard for the rights, safety and health of tenants and others lawfully on the premises. (Adopted 1/95, Amended 1/00)

• Standard of Practice 1-11

REALTORS® who are employed to maintain or manage a client's property shall exercise due diligence and make reasonable efforts to protect it against reasonably foreseeable contingencies and losses. (Adopted 1/95)

• Standard of Practice 1-12

When entering into listing contracts, REALTORS® must advise sellers/landlords of:

1) the REALTOR®'s company policies regarding cooperation and the amount(s) of any compensation that will be offered to subagents, buyer/tenant agents, and/or brokers acting in legally recognized non-agency capacities;

2) the fact that buyer/tenant agents or brokers, even if compensated by listing brokers, or by sellers/landlords may represent the interests of buyers/tenants; and

3) any potential for listing brokers to act as disclosed dual agents, e.g. buyer/tenant agents. (Adopted 1/93, Renumbered 1/98, Amended 1/03)

• Standard of Practice 1-13

When entering into buyer/tenant agreements, REALTORS® must advise potential clients of:

1) the REALTOR®'s company policies regarding cooperation;

2) the amount of compensation to be paid by the client;

3) the potential for additional or offsetting compensation from other brokers, from the seller or landlord, or from other parties;

4) any potential for the buyer/tenant representative to act as a disclosed dual agent, e.g. listing broker, subagent, landlord's agent, etc., and

5) the possibility that sellers or sellers' representatives may not treat the existence, terms, or conditions of offers as confidential unless confidentiality is required by law, regulation, or by any confidentiality agreement between the parties. (Adopted 1/93, Renumbered 1/98, Amended 1/06)

• Standard of Practice 1-14

Fees for preparing appraisals or other valuations shall not be contingent upon the amount of the appraisal or valuation. (Adopted 1/02)

• Standard of Practice 1-15

REALTORS®, in response to inquiries from buyers or cooperating brokers shall, with the sellers' approval, disclose the existence of offers on the property. Where disclosure is authorized, REALTORS® shall also disclose whether offers were obtained by the listing licensee, another licensee in the listing firm, or by a cooperating broker. (Adopted 1/03, Amended 1/06)

Article 2

REALTORS® shall avoid exaggeration, misrepresentation, or concealment of pertinent facts relating to the property or the transaction. REALTORS® shall not, however, be obligated to discover latent defects in the property, to advise on matters outside the scope of their real estate license, or to disclose facts which are confidential under the scope of agency or non-agency relationships as defined by state law. (Amended 1/00)

• Standard of Practice 2-1

REALTORS® shall only be obligated to discover and disclose adverse factors reasonably apparent to someone with expertise in those areas required by their real estate licensing authority. Article 2 does not impose upon the REALTOR® the obligation of expertise in other professional or technical disciplines. (Amended 1/96)

• Standard of Practice 2-2

(Renumbered as Standard of Practice 1-12 1/98)

• Standard of Practice 2-3

(Renumbered as Standard of Practice 1-13 1/98)

• Standard of Practice 2-4

REALTORS® shall not be parties to the naming of a false consideration in any document, unless it be the naming of an obviously nominal consideration.

• Standard of Practice 2-5

Factors defined as "non-material" by law or regulation or which are expressly referenced in law or regulation as not being subject to disclosure are considered not "pertinent" for purposes of Article 2. (Adopted 1/93)

Article 3

REALTORS® shall cooperate with other brokers except when cooperation is not in the client's best interest. The obligation to cooperate does not include the obligation to share commissions, fees, or to otherwise compensate another broker. (Amended 1/95)

• Standard of Practice 3-1

REALTORS®, acting as exclusive agents or brokers of sellers/ landlords, establish the terms and conditions of offers to cooperate. Unless expressly indicated in offers to cooperate, cooperating brokers may not assume that the offer of cooperation includes an offer of compensation. Terms of compensation, if any, shall be ascertained by cooperating brokers before beginning efforts to accept the offer of cooperation. (Amended 1/99)

• Standard of Practice 3-2

REALTORS® shall, with respect to offers of compensation to another REALTOR®, timely communicate any change of compensation for cooperative services to the other REALTOR® prior to the time such REALTOR® produces an offer to purchase/lease the property. (Amended 1/94)

• Standard of Practice 3-3

Standard of Practice 3-2 does not preclude the listing broker and cooperating broker from entering into an agreement to change cooperative compensation. (Adopted 1/94)

• Standard of Practice 3-4

REALTORS®, acting as listing brokers, have an affirmative obligation to disclose the existence of dual or variable rate commission arrangements (i.e., listings where one amount of commission is payable if the listing broker's firm is the procuring cause of sale/lease and a different amount of commission is payable if the sale/lease results through the efforts of the seller/landlord or a cooperating broker). The listing broker shall, as soon as practical, disclose the existence of such arrangements to potential cooperating brokers and shall, in response to inquiries from cooperating brokers, disclose the differential that would result in a cooperative transaction or in a sale/lease that results through the efforts of the seller/landlord. If the cooperating broker is a buyer/tenant representative, the buyer/tenant representative must disclose such information to their client before the client makes an offer to purchase or lease. (Amended 1/02)

• Standard of Practice 3-5

It is the obligation of subagents to promptly disclose all pertinent facts to the principal's agent prior to as well as after a purchase or lease agreement is executed. (Amended 1/93)

• Standard of Practice 3-6

REALTORS® shall disclose the existence of accepted offers, including offers with unresolved contingencies, to any broker seeking cooperation. (Adopted 5/86, Amended 1/04)

• Standard of Practice 3-7

When seeking information from another REALTOR® concerning property under a management or listing agreement, REALTORS® shall disclose their REALTOR® status and whether their interest is personal or on behalf of a client and, if on behalf of a client, their representational status. (Amended 1/95)

• Standard of Practice 3-8
REALTORS® shall not misrepresent the availability of access to show or inspect a listed property. (Amended 11/87)

Article 4
REALTORS® shall not acquire an interest in or buy or present offers from themselves, any member of their immediate families, their firms or any member thereof, or any entities in which they have any ownership interest, any real property without making their true position known to the owner or the owner's agent or broker. In selling property they own, or in which they have any interest, REALTORS® shall reveal their ownership or interest in writing to the purchaser or the purchaser's representative. (Amended 1/00)

• Standard of Practice 4-1
For the protection of all parties, the disclosures required by Article 4 shall be in writing and provided by REALTORS® prior to the signing of any contract. (Adopted 2/86)

Article 5
REALTORS® shall not undertake to provide professional services concerning a property or its value where they have a present or contemplated interest unless such interest is specifically disclosed to all affected parties.

Article 6
REALTORS® shall not accept any commission, rebate, or profit on

expenditures made for their client, without the client's knowledge and consent.

When recommending real estate products or services (e.g., homeowner's insurance, warranty programs, mortgage financing, title insurance, etc.), REALTORS® shall disclose to the client or customer to whom the recommendation is made any financial benefits or fees, other than real estate referral fees, the REALTOR® or REALTOR®'s firm may receive as a direct result of such recommendation. (Amended 1/99)

• Standard of Practice 6-1

REALTORS® shall not recommend or suggest to a client or a customer the use of services of another organization or business entity in which they have a direct interest without disclosing such interest at the time of the recommendation or suggestion. (Amended 5/88)

Article 7

In a transaction, REALTORS® shall not accept compensation from more than one party, even if permitted by law, without disclosure to all parties and the informed consent of the REALTOR®'s client or clients. (Amended 1/93)

Article 8

REALTORS® shall keep in a special account in an appropriate financial institution, separated from their own funds, monies coming into their possession in trust for other persons, such as escrows, trust funds, clients' monies, and other like items.

Article 9

REALTORS®, for the protection of all parties, shall assure whenever possible that all agreements related to real estate transactions including, but not limited to, listing and representation agreements, purchase contracts, and leases are in writing in clear and understandable language expressing the specific terms, conditions, obligations and commitments of the parties. A copy of each agreement shall be furnished to each party to such agreements upon their signing or initialing. (Amended 1/04)

• Standard of Practice 9-1

For the protection of all parties, REALTORS® shall use reasonable care to ensure that documents pertaining to the purchase, sale, or lease of real estate are kept current through the use of written extensions or amendments. (Amended 1/93)

Duties to the Public

Article 10

REALTORS® shall not deny equal professional services to any person for reasons of race, color, religion, sex, handicap, familial status, or national origin. REALTORS® shall not be parties to any plan or agreement to discriminate against a person or persons on the basis of race, color, religion, sex, handicap, familial status, or national origin. (Amended 1/90)

REALTORS®, in their real estate employment practices, shall not discriminate against any person or persons on the basis of race, color, religion, sex, handicap, familial status, or national origin. (Amended 1/00)

• Standard of Practice 10-1

When involved in the sale or lease of a residence, REALTORS® shall not volunteer information regarding the racial, religious or ethnic composition of any neighborhood nor shall they engage in any activity which may result in panic selling, however, REALTORS® may provide other demographic information. (Adopted 1/94, Amended 1/06)

• Standard of Practice 10-2

When not involved in the sale or lease of a residence, REALTORS® may provide demographic information related to a property, transaction or professional assignment to a party if such demographic information is (a) deemed by the REALTOR® to be needed to assist with or complete, in a manner consistent with Article 10, a real estate transaction or professional assignment and (b) is obtained or derived from a recognized, reliable, independent, and impartial source. The source of such information and any additions, deletions, modifications, interpretations, or other changes shall be disclosed in reasonable detail. (Adopted 1/05, Renumbered 1/06)

• Standard of Practice 10-3

REALTORS® shall not print, display or circulate any statement or advertisement with respect to selling or renting of a property that indicates any preference, limitations or discrimination based on race, color, religion, sex, handicap, familial status, or national origin. (Adopted 1/94, Renumbered 1/05 and 1/06)

• Standard of Practice 10-4

As used in Article 10 "real estate employment practices" relates to employees and independent contractors providing real estate-related services and the administrative and clerical staff directly supporting those individuals. (Adopted 1/00, Renumbered 1/05 and 1/06)

Article 11

The services which REALTORS® provide to their clients and customers shall conform to the standards of practice and competence which are reasonably expected in the specific real estate disciplines in which they engage; specifically, residential real estate brokerage, real property management, commercial and industrial real estate brokerage, real estate appraisal, real estate counseling, real estate syndication, real estate auction, and international real estate.

REALTORS® shall not undertake to provide specialized professional services concerning a type of property or service that is outside their field of competence unless they engage the assistance of one who is competent on such types of property or service, or unless the facts are fully disclosed to the client. Any persons engaged to provide such assistance shall be so identified to the client and their contribution to the assignment should be set forth. (Amended 1/95)

• **Standard of Practice 11-1**
When REALTORS® prepare opinions of real property value or price, other than in pursuit of a listing or to assist a potential purchaser in formulating a purchase offer, such opinions shall include the following:

1) identification of the subject property

2) date prepared

3) defined value or price

4) limiting conditions, including statements of purpose(s) and intended user(s)

5) any present or contemplated interest, including the possibility of representing the seller/landlord or buyers/tenants

6) basis for the opinion, including applicable market data

7) if the opinion is not an appraisal, a statement to that effect (Amended 1/01)

• Standard of Practice 11-2

The obligations of the Code of Ethics in respect of real estate disciplines other than appraisal shall be interpreted and applied in accordance with the standards of competence and practice which clients and the public reasonably require to protect their rights and interests considering the complexity of the transaction, the availability of expert assistance, and, where the REALTOR® is an agent or subagent, the obligations of a fiduciary. (Adopted 1/95)

• Standard of Practice 11-3

When REALTORS® provide consultive services to clients which involve advice or counsel for a fee (not a commission), such advice shall be rendered in an objective manner and the fee shall not be contingent on the substance of the advice or counsel given. If brokerage or transaction services are to be provided in addition to consultive services, a separate compensation may be paid with prior agreement between the client and REALTOR®. (Adopted 1/96)

• Standard of Practice 11-4

The competency required by Article 11 relates to services contracted for between REALTORS® and their clients or customers; the duties expressly imposed by the Code of Ethics; and the duties imposed by law or regulation. (Adopted 1/02)

Article 12

REALTORS® shall be careful at all times to present a true picture in their advertising and representations to the public. REALTORS® shall also ensure that their professional status (e.g., broker, appraiser, property manager, etc.) or status as REALTORS® is clearly identifiable in any such advertising. (Amended 1/93)

• Standard of Practice 12-1

REALTORS® may use the term "free" and similar terms in their advertising and in other representations provided that all terms governing availability of the offered product or service are clearly disclosed at the same time. (Amended 1/97)

• Standard of Practice 12-2

REALTORS® may represent their services as "free" or without cost even if they expect to receive compensation from a source other than their client provided that the potential for the REALTOR® to obtain a benefit from a third party is clearly disclosed at the same time. (Amended 1/97)

• Standard of Practice 12-3

The offering of premiums, prizes, merchandise discounts or other inducements to list, sell, purchase, or lease is not, in itself, unethical even if receipt of the benefit is contingent on listing, selling, purchasing, or leasing through the REALTOR® making the offer. However, REALTORS® must exercise care and candor in any such advertising or other public or private representations so that any party interested in receiving or otherwise benefiting from the REALTOR®'s offer will have clear, thorough, advance understanding of all the terms and conditions of the offer. The offering of any inducements to do business is subject to the limitations and restrictions of state law and the ethical obligations established by any applicable Standard of Practice. (Amended 1/95)

• Standard of Practice 12-4

REALTORS® shall not offer for sale/lease or advertise property without authority. When acting as listing brokers or as subagents, REALTORS® shall not quote a price different from that agreed upon with the seller/landlord. (Amended 1/93)

• Standard of Practice 12-5

REALTORS® shall not advertise nor permit any person employed by or affiliated with them to advertise listed property without disclosing the name of the firm. (Adopted 11/86)

• Standard of Practice 12-6

REALTORS®, when advertising unlisted real property for sale/lease in which they have an ownership interest, shall disclose their status as both owners/landlords and as REALTORS® or real estate licensees. (Amended 1/93)

• Standard of Practice 12-7

Only REALTORS® who participated in the transaction as the listing broker or cooperating broker (selling broker) may claim to have "sold" the property. Prior to closing, a cooperating broker may post a "sold" sign only with the consent of the listing broker. (Amended 1/96)

Article 13

REALTORS® shall not engage in activities that constitute the unauthorized practice of law and shall recommend that legal counsel be obtained when the interest of any party to the transaction requires it.

Article 14

If charged with unethical practice or asked to present evidence or to cooperate in any other way, in any professional standards proceeding or investigation, REALTORS® shall place all pertinent facts before the proper tribunals of the Member Board or affiliated institute, society, or council in which membership is held and shall take no action to disrupt or obstruct such processes. (Amended 1/99)

• Standard of Practice 14-1

REALTORS® shall not be subject to disciplinary proceedings in more than one Board of REALTORS® or affiliated institute, society or council in which they hold membership with respect to alleged violations of the Code of Ethics relating to the same transaction or event. (Amended 1/95)

• Standard of Practice 14-2

REALTORS® shall not make any unauthorized disclosure or dissemination of the allegations, findings, or decision developed in connection with an ethics hearing or appeal or in connection with an arbitration hearing or procedural review. (Amended 1/92)

• Standard of Practice 14-3

REALTORS® shall not obstruct the Board's investigative or professional standards proceedings by instituting or threatening to institute actions for libel, slander or defamation against any party to a professional standards proceeding or their witnesses based on the filing of an arbitration request, an ethics complaint, or testimony given before any tribunal. (Adopted 11/87, Amended 1/99)

• Standard of Practice 14-4

REALTORS® shall not intentionally impede the Board's investigative or disciplinary proceedings by filing multiple ethics complaints based on the same event or transaction. (Adopted 11/88)

Duties to the REALTORS®

Article 15

REALTORS® shall not knowingly or recklessly make false or misleading statements about competitors, their businesses, or their business practices. (Amended 1/92)

• Standard of Practice 15-1

REALTORS® shall not knowingly or recklessly file false or unfounded ethics complaints. (Adopted 1/00)

Article 16

REALTORS® shall not engage in any practice or take any action inconsistent with exclusive representation or exclusive brokerage relationship agreements that other REALTORS® have with clients. (Amended 1/04)

• Standard of Practice 16-1

Article 16 is not intended to prohibit aggressive or innovative business practices which are otherwise ethical and does not prohibit disagreements with other REALTORS® involving commission, fees, compensation or other forms of payment or expenses. (Adopted 1/93, Amended 1/95)

• Standard of Practice 16-2

Article 16 does not preclude REALTORS® from making general announcements to prospects describing their services and the terms of their availability even though some recipients may have entered into agency agreements or other exclusive relationships with another REALTOR®. A general telephone canvass, general mailing or distribution addressed to all prospects in a given geographical area or in a given profession, business, club, or organization, or other classification or group is deemed "general" for purposes of this standard. (Amended 1/04)

Article 16 is intended to recognize as unethical two basic types of solicitations:

First, telephone or personal solicitations of property owners who have been identified by a real estate sign, multiple listing compilation, or other information service as having exclusively listed their property with another REALTOR®; and

Second, mail or other forms of written solicitations of prospects whose properties are exclusively listed with another REALTOR® when such solicitations are not part of a general mailing but are directed specifically to property owners identified through compilations of current listings, "for sale" or "for rent" signs, or other sources of information required by Article 3 and Multiple Listing Service rules to be made available to other REALTORS® under offers of subagency or cooperation. (Amended 1/04)

• Standard of Practice 16-3

Article 16 does not preclude REALTORS® from contacting the client of another broker for the purpose of offering to provide, or entering into a contract to provide, a different type of real estate service unrelated to the type of service currently being provided (e.g., property management as opposed to brokerage) or from offering the same type of service for property not subject to other brokers' exclusive agreements. However, information received through a Multiple Listing Service or any other offer of cooperation may not be used to target clients of other REALTORS® to whom such offers to provide services may be made. (Amended 1/04)

• Standard of Practice 16-4

REALTORS® shall not solicit a listing which is currently listed exclusively with another broker. However, if the listing broker, when asked by the REALTOR®, refuses to disclose the expiration date and nature of such listing; i.e., an exclusive right to sell, an exclusive agency, open listing, or other form of contractual agreement between the listing broker and the client, the REALTOR® may contact the owner to secure such information and may discuss the terms upon which the REALTOR® might take a future listing or, alternatively, may take a listing to become effective upon expiration of any existing exclusive listing. (Amended 1/94)

• Standard of Practice 16-5

REALTORS® shall not solicit buyer/tenant agreements from buyers/ tenants who are subject to exclusive buyer/tenant agreements. However, if asked by a REALTOR®, the broker refuses to disclose the expiration date of the exclusive buyer/tenant agreement, the REALTOR® may contact the buyer/tenant to secure such information and may discuss the terms upon which the REALTOR® might enter into a future buyer/tenant agreement or, alternatively, may enter into a buyer/tenant agreement to become effective upon the expiration of any existing exclusive buyer/tenant agreement. (Adopted 1/94, Amended 1/98)

• Standard of Practice 16-6

When REALTORS® are contacted by the client of another REALTOR® regarding the creation of an exclusive relationship to provide the same type of service, and REALTORS® have not directly or indirectly initiated such discussions, they may discuss the terms upon which they might enter into a future agreement or, alternatively, may enter into an agreement which becomes effective upon expiration of any existing exclusive agreement. (Amended 1/98)

• Standard of Practice 16-7

The fact that a prospect has retained a REALTOR® as an exclusive representative or exclusive broker in one or more past transactions does not preclude other REALTORS® from seeking such prospect's future business. (Amended 1/04)

• Standard of Practice 16-8

The fact that an exclusive agreement has been entered into with a REALTOR® shall not preclude or inhibit any other REALTOR® from entering into a similar agreement after the expiration of the prior agreement. (Amended 1/98)

• Standard of Practice 16-9

REALTORS®, prior to entering into a representation agreement, have an affirmative obligation to make reasonable efforts to determine whether the prospect is subject to a current, valid exclusive agreement to provide the same type of real estate service. (Amended 1/04)

• Standard of Practice 16-10

REALTORS®, acting as buyer or tenant representatives or brokers, shall disclose that relationship to the seller/landlord's representative or broker at first contact and shall provide written confirmation of that disclosure to the seller/ landlord's representative or broker not later than execution of a purchase agreement or lease. (Amended 1/04)

• Standard of Practice 16-11

On unlisted property, REALTORS® acting as buyer/tenant representatives or brokers shall disclose that relationship to the seller/landlord at first contact for that buyer/tenant and shall provide written confirmation of such disclosure to the seller/landlord not later than execution of any purchase or lease agreement. (Amended 1/04)

REALTORS® shall make any request for anticipated compensation from the seller/landlord at first contact. (Amended 1/98)

• Standard of Practice 16-12

REALTORS®, acting as representatives or brokers of sellers/landlords or as subagents of listing brokers, shall disclose that relationship to buyers/tenants as soon as practicable and shall provide written confirmation of such disclosure to buyers/tenants not later than execution of any purchase or lease agreement. (Amended 1/04)

• Standard of Practice 16-13

All dealings concerning property exclusively listed, or with buyer/ tenants who are subject to an exclusive agreement shall be carried on with the client's representative or broker, and not with the client, except with the consent of the client's representative or broker or except where such dealings are initiated by the client.

Before providing substantive services (such as writing a purchase offer or presenting a CMA) to prospects, REALTORS® shall ask prospects whether they are a party to any exclusive representation agreement. REALTORS® shall not knowingly provide substantive services concerning a prospective transaction to prospects who are parties to exclusive representation agreements, except with the consent of the prospects' exclusive representatives or at the direction of prospects. (Adopted 1/93, Amended 1/04)

• Standard of Practice 16-14

REALTORS® are free to enter into contractual relationships or to negotiate with sellers/ landlords, buyers/tenants or others who are not subject to an exclusive agreement but shall not knowingly obligate them to pay more than one commission except with their informed consent. (Amended 1/98)

• Standard of Practice 16-15

In cooperative transactions REALTORS® shall compensate cooperating REALTORS® (principal brokers) and shall not compensate nor offer to compensate, directly or indirectly, any of the sales licensees employed by or affiliated with other REALTORS® without the prior express knowledge and consent of the cooperating broker.

• Standard of Practice 16-16

REALTORS®, acting as subagents or buyer/tenant representatives or brokers, shall not use the terms of an offer to purchase/lease to attempt to modify the listing broker's offer of compensation to subagents or buyer/tenant representatives or brokers nor make the submission of an executed offer to purchase/lease contingent on the listing broker's agreement to modify the offer of compensation. (Amended 1/04)

• Standard of Practice 16-17
REALTORS®, acting as subagents or as buyer/tenant representatives or brokers, shall not attempt to extend a listing broker's offer of cooperation and/or compensation to other brokers without the consent of the listing broker. (Amended 1/04)

• Standard of Practice 16-18
REALTORS® shall not use information obtained from listing brokers through offers to cooperate made through multiple listing services or through other offers of cooperation to refer listing brokers' clients to other brokers or to create buyer/tenant relationships with listing brokers' clients, unless such use is authorized by listing brokers. (Amended 1/02)

• Standard of Practice 16-19
Signs giving notice of property for sale, rent, lease, or exchange shall not be placed on property without consent of the seller/landlord. (Amended 1/93)

• Standard of Practice 16-20
REALTORS®, prior to or after terminating their relationship with their current firm, shall not induce clients of their current firm to cancel exclusive contractual agreements between the client and that firm. This does not preclude REALTORS® (principals) from establishing agreements with their ASSOCIATEd licensees governing assignability of exclusive agreements. (Adopted 1/98)

Article 17

In the event of contractual disputes or specific non-contractual disputes as defined in Standard of Practice 17-4 between REALTORS® (principals) ASSOCIATEd with different firms, arising out of their relationship as REALTORS®, the REALTORS® shall submit the dispute to arbitration in accordance with the regulations of their Board or Boards rather than litigate the matter.

In the event clients of REALTORS® wish to arbitrate contractual disputes arising out of real estate transactions, REALTORS® shall arbitrate those disputes in accordance with the regulations of their Board, provided the clients agree to be bound by the decision.

The obligation to participate in arbitration contemplated by this Article includes the obligation of REALTORS® (principals) to cause their firms to arbitrate and be bound by any award. (Amended 1/01)

• Standard of Practice 17-1
The filing of litigation and refusal to withdraw from it by REALTORS® in an arbitrable matter constitutes a refusal to arbitrate. (Adopted 2/86)

• Standard of Practice 17-2
Article 17 does not require REALTORS® to arbitrate in those circumstances when all parties to the dispute advise the Board in writing that they choose not to arbitrate before the Board.
(Amended 1/93)

• Standard of Practice 17-3
REALTORS®, when acting solely as principals in a real estate transaction, are not obligated to arbitrate disputes with other REALTORS® absent a specific written agreement to the contrary. (Adopted 1/96)

• Standard of Practice 17-4

Specific non-contractual disputes that are subject to arbitration pursuant to Article 17 are:

1) Where a listing broker has compensated a cooperating broker and another cooperating broker subsequently claims to be the procuring cause of the sale or lease. In such cases the complainant may name the first cooperating broker as respondent and arbitration may proceed without the listing broker being named as a respondent. Alternatively, if the complaint is brought against the listing broker, the listing broker may name the first cooperating broker as a third-party respondent. In either instance the decision of the hearing panel as to procuring cause shall be conclusive with respect to all current or subsequent claims of the parties for compensation arising out of the underlying cooperative transaction. (Adopted 1/97)

2) Where a buyer or tenant representative is compensated by the seller or landlord, and not by the listing broker, and the listing broker, as a result, reduces the commission owed by the seller or landlord and, subsequent to such actions, another cooperating broker claims to be the procuring cause of sale or lease. In such cases the complainant may name the first cooperating broker as respondent and arbitration may proceed without the listing broker being named as a respondent. Alternatively, if the complaint is brought against the listing broker, the listing broker may name the first cooperating broker as a third-party respondent. In either instance the decision of the hearing panel as to procuring cause shall be conclusive with respect to all current or subsequent claims of the parties for compensation arising out of the underlying cooperative transaction. (Adopted 1/97)

3) Where a buyer or tenant representative is compensated by the buyer or tenant and, as a result, the listing broker reduces the commission

owed by the seller or landlord and, subsequent to such actions, another cooperating broker claims to be the procuring cause of sale or lease. In such cases the complainant may name the first cooperating broker as respondent and arbitration may proceed without the listing broker being named as a respondent. Alternatively, if the complaint is brought against the listing broker, the listing broker may name the first cooperating broker as a third-party respondent. In either instance the decision of the hearing panel as to procuring cause shall be conclusive with respect to all current or subsequent claims of the parties for compensation arising out of the underlying cooperative transaction. (Adopted 1/97)

4) Where two or more listing brokers claim entitlement to compensation pursuant to open listings with a seller or landlord who agrees to participate in arbitration (or who requests arbitration) and who agrees to be bound by the decision. In cases where one of the listing brokers has been compensated by the seller or landlord, the other listing broker, as complainant, may name the first listing broker as respondent and arbitration may proceed between the brokers. (Adopted 1/97)

5) Where a buyer or tenant representative is compensated by the seller or landlord, and not by the listing broker, and the listing broker, as a result, reduces the commission owed by the seller or landlord and, subsequent to such actions, claims to be the procuring cause of sale or lease. In such cases arbitration shall be between the listing broker and the buyer or tenant representative and the amount in dispute is limited to the amount of the reduction of commission to which the listing broker agreed. (Adopted 1/05)

The Code of Ethics was adopted in 1913. Amended at the Annual Convention in 1924, 1928, 1950, 1951, 1952, 1955, 1956, 1961, 1962, 1974, 1982, 1986, 1987, 1989, 1990, 1991, 1992, 1993, 1994, 1995,

1996, 1997, 1998, 1999, 2000, 2001, 2002, 2003, 2004 and 2005.

Explanatory Notes

The reader should be aware of the following policies which have been approved by the Board of Directors of the National Association:

In filing a charge of an alleged violation of the Code of Ethics by a REALTOR®, the charge must read as an alleged violation of one or more Articles of the Code. Standards of Practice may be cited in support of the charge.

The Standards of Practice serve to clarify the ethical obligations imposed by the various Articles and supplement, and do not substitute for, the Case Interpretations in Interpretations of the Code of Ethics.

Modifications to existing Standards of Practice and additional new Standards of Practice are approved from time to time. Readers are cautioned to ensure that the most recent publications are utilized.

APPENDIX 3

Regulation Z
Truth in Lending Act

Laws and Regulations

In the world of mortgage and real estate there are many laws, regulations and rules and these standards have been set in place for specific reasons, most importantly to keep a sense of fair play and protection for all. As in most cases there are always the loop holes and cheaters that devise new and inventive ways to evade these standards for their own personal gains. It would seem that as soon as a law of prevention is created that three new ways to cheat that law are devised. It is a never-ending battle.

Keep in mind that many states have adopted revisions to these laws as they deem necessary.

The Truth in Lending Act (TILA), Title I of the Consumer Credit Protection Act, is aimed at promoting the informed use of consumer credit by requiring disclosures about its terms and costs. In general, this regulation applies to each individual or business that offers or extends credit when the credit is offered or extended to consumers; the credit is subject to a finance charge or is payable by a written agreement in more than four installments; the credit is primarily for personal, family or household purposes; and the loan balance equals or exceeds $25,000 or is secured by an interest in real property or a dwelling.

TILA is intended to enable the customer to compare the cost of cash versus credit transaction and the difference in the cost of credit among different lenders. The regulation also requires a maximum interest rate to be stated in variable rate contracts secured by the borrower's dwelling, imposes limitations on home equity plans that are subject to the requirements of certain sections of the Act and requires a maximum interest that may apply during the term of a mortgage loan. TILA also establishes disclosure standards for advertisements that refer to certain credit terms.

In addition to financial disclosure, TILA provides consumers with substantive rights in connection with certain types of credit transactions to which it relates, including a right of rescission in certain real estate lending transactions, regulation of certain credit card practices and a means for fair and timely resolution of credit billing disputes. This discussion will be limited to those provisions of TILA that relate specifically to the mortgage lending process, including:

1. **Early and Final Regulation Z Disclosure Requirements**
2. **Disclosure Requirements for ARM Loans**
3. **Right of Rescission**
4. **Advertising Disclosure Requirements**

Early and Final Regulation Z Disclosure Requirements:

TILA requires lenders to make certain disclosures on loans subject to the Real Estate Settlement Procedures Act (RESPA) within three business days after their receipt of a written application. This early disclosure statement is partially based on the initial information provided by the consumer. A final disclosure statement is provided at the time of loan closing. The disclosure is required to be in a specific format and include the following information:

1. Name and address of creditor
2. Amount financed
3. Itemization of amount financed (optional, if Good Faith Estimate is provided)
4. Finance charge
5. Annual percentage rate (APR)
6. Variable rate information
7. Payment schedule
8. Total of payments
9. Demand feature
10. Total sales price
11. Prepayment policy
12. Late payment policy
13. Security interest
14. Insurance requirements
15. Certain security interest charges
16. Contract reference
17. Assumption policy
18. Required deposit information

Disclosure Requirements for ARM Loans:

If the annual percentage rate on a loan secured by the consumer's principal dwelling may increase after consummation and the term of the loan exceeds one year, TILA requires additional adjustable rate mortgage disclosures to be provided, including:

- The booklet titled Consumer Handbook on Adjustable Rate Mortgages, published by the Board and the Federal Home Loan Bank Board or a suitable substitute.
- A loan program disclosure for each variable-rate program in which the consumer expresses an interest. The loan program disclosure shall contain the necessary information as prescribed

by Regulation Z.

TILA requires servicers to provide subsequent disclosure to consumers on variable rate transactions in each month an interest rate adjustment takes place.

Right of Rescission:

In a credit transaction in which a security interest is or will be retained or acquired in a consumer's principal dwelling, each consumer whose ownership is or will be subject to the security interest has the right to rescind the transaction. Lenders are required to deliver two copies of the notice of the right to rescind and one copy of the disclosure statement to each consumer entitled to rescind. The notice must be on a separate document that identifies the rescission period on the transaction and must clearly and conspicuously disclose the retention or acquisition of a security interest in the consumer's principal dwelling; the consumer's right to rescind the transaction; and how the consumer may exercise the right to rescind with a form for that purpose, designating the address of the lender's place of business.

In order to exercise the right to rescind, the consumer must notify the creditor of the rescission by mail, telegram or other means of communication. Notice is considered given when mailed, filed for telegraphic transmission or sent by other means, when delivered to the lender's designated place of business. The consumer may exercise the right to rescind until midnight of the third business day following consummation of the transaction; delivery of the notice of right to rescind; or delivery of all material disclosures, whichever occurs last. When more than one consumer in a transaction has the right to rescind, the exercise of the right by one consumer shall be effective for all consumers.

When a consumer rescinds a transaction, the security interest giving rise to the right of rescission becomes void and the consumer will no longer be liable for any amount, including any finance charge. Within 20 calendar days after receipt of a notice of rescission, the lender is required to return any money or property that was given to anyone in connection with the transaction and must take any action necessary to reflect the termination of the security interest. If the lender has delivered any money or property, the consumer may retain possession until the lender has complied with the above.

The consumer may modify or waive the right to rescind if the consumer determines that the extension of credit is needed to meet a bona fide personal financial emergency. To modify or waive the right, the consumer must give the lender a dated written statement that describes the emergency, specifically modifies or waives the right to rescind and bears the signature of all of the consumers entitled to rescind. Printed forms for this purpose are prohibited.

Advertising Disclosure Requirements:

If a lender advertises directly to a consumer, TILA requires the advertisement to disclose the credit terms and rate in a certain manner. If an advertisement for credit states specific credit terms, it may state only those terms that actually are or will be arranged or offered by the lender. If an advertisement states a rate of finance charge, it may state the rate as an "annual percentage rate" (APR) using that term. If the annual percentage rate may be increased after consummation the advertisement must state that fact. The advertisement may not state any other rate, except that a simple annual rate or periodic rate that is applied to an unpaid balance may be stated in conjunction with, but not more conspicuously than, the annual percentage rate.

Subpart A—General (from www.fdic.gov)

§ 226.1 Authority, purpose, coverage, organization, enforcement and liability.

(a) Authority. This regulation, known as Regulation Z, is issued by the Board of Governors of the Federal Reserve System to implement the federal Truth in Lending Act, which is contained in title I of the Consumer Credit Protection Act, as amended (15 U.S.C. 1601 et seq.). This regulation also implements title XII, section 1204 of the Competitive Equality Banking Act of 1987 (Pub. L. 100--86, 101 Stat. 552). Information-collection requirements contained in this regulation have been approved by the Office of Management and Budget under the provisions of 44 U.S.C. 3501 et seq. and have been assigned OMB No. 7100--0199.

(b) Purpose. The purpose of this regulation is to promote the informed use of consumer credit by requiring disclosures about its terms and cost. The regulation also gives consumers the right to cancel certain credit transactions that involve a lien on a consumer's principal dwelling, regulates certain credit card practices, and provides a means for fair and timely resolution of credit billing disputes. The regulation does not govern charges for consumer credit. The regulation requires a maximum interest rate to be stated in variable-rate contracts secured by the consumer's dwelling. It also imposes limitations on home equity plans that are subject to the requirements of § 226.5b and mortgages that are subject to the requirements of § 226.32. The regulation prohibits certain acts or practices in connection with credit secured by a consumer's principal dwelling.

(c) Coverage. (1) In general, this regulation applies to each individual or business that offers or extends credit when four conditions are met:

(i) the credit is offered or extended to consumers; (ii) the offering or extension of credit is done regularly; [1] (iii) the credit is subject to a finance charge or is payable by a written agreement in more than 4 installments; and (iv) the credit is primarily for personal, family, or household purposes.

(2) If a credit card is involved, however, certain provisions apply even if the credit is not subject to a finance charge, or is not payable by a written agreement in more than 4 installments, or if the credit card is to be used for business purposes.

(3) In addition, certain requirements of § 226.5b apply to persons who are not creditors but who provide applications for home equity plans to consumers.

(d) Organization. The regulation is divided into subparts and appendices as follows:

(1) Subpart A contains general information. It sets forth: (i) the authority, purpose, coverage, and organization of the regulation; (ii) the definitions of basic terms; (iii) the transactions that are exempt from coverage; and (iv) the method of determining the finance charge.

(2) Subpart B contains the rules for open-end credit. It requires that initial disclosures and periodic statements be provided, as well as additional disclosures for credit and charge card applications and solicitations and for home equity plans subject to the requirements of §§ 226.5a and 226.5b, respectively. It also describes special rules that apply to credit card transactions, treatment of payments and credit balances, procedures for resolving credit billing errors, annual percentage rate calculations, rescission requirements, and advertising rules.

{{12-31-01 p.6643}}

(3) Subpart C relates to closed-end credit. It contains rules on disclosures, treatment of credit balances, annual percentage rate calculations, rescission requirements, and advertising.

(4) Subpart D contains rules on oral disclosures, Spanish language

disclosure in Puerto Rico, record retention, effect on state laws, state exemptions, and rate limitations.

(5) Subpart E contains special rules for mortgage transactions. Section 226.32 requires certain disclosures and provides limitations for loans that have rates and fees above specified amounts. Section 226.33 requires disclosures, including the total annual loan cost rate, for reverse mortgage transactions. Section 226.34 prohibits specific acts and practices in connection with mortgage transactions.

(6) Several appendices contain information such as the procedures for determinations about state laws, state exemptions and issuance of staff interpretations, special rules for certain kinds of credit plans, a list of enforcement agencies, and the rules for computing annual percentage rates in closed-end credit transactions and total annual loan cost rates for reverse mortgage transactions.

(e) Enforcement and liability. Section 108 of the act contains the administrative enforcement provisions. Sections 112, 113, 130, 131, and 134 contain provisions relating to liability for failure to comply with the requirements of the act and the regulation. Section 1204(c) of Title XII of the Competitive Equality Banking Act of 1987, Pub. L. No. 100--86, 101 Stat. 552, incorporates by reference administrative enforcement and civil liability provisions of sections 108 and 130 of the act.

[Codified to 12 C.F.R. § 226.1]

[Section 226.1 amended at 49 Fed. Reg. 46991, November 30, 1984, effective December 31, 1984; 52 Fed. Reg. 43181, November 9, 1987, effective December 9, 1987; 54 Fed. Reg. 13865, April 6, 1989, effective April 3, 1989, but compliance is optional until August 31, 1989; 54 Fed. Reg. 24686, June 9, 1989, effective June 7, 1989, but compliance is optional until November 7, 1989; 60 Fed. Reg. 15471, March 24, 1995, effective March 22, 1995, compliance is optional until October 1, 1995; 66 Fed. Reg. 65617, December 20, 2001, effective December 20, 2001, but compliance is mandatory as of October 1, 2002]

§ 226.2 Definitions and rules of construction.

(a) Definitions. For purposes of this regulation, the following definitions apply:

(1) Act means the Truth in Lending Act (15 U.S.C. 1601 et seq.).

(2) Advertisement means a commercial message in any medium that promotes, directly or indirectly, a credit transaction.

(3) [Reserved] [2]

(4) Billing cycle or cycle means the interval between the days or dates of regular periodic statements. These intervals shall be equal and no longer than a quarter of a year. An interval will be considered equal if the number of days in the cycle does not vary more than four days from the regular day or date of the periodic statement.

(5) Board means the Board of Governors of the Federal Reserve System.

(6) Business day means a day on which a creditor's offices are open to the public for carrying on substantially all of its business functions. However, for purposes of rescission under §§ 226.15 and 226.23, and for purposes of § 226.31, the term means all calendar days except Sundays and the legal public holidays specified in 5 U.S.C. 6103(a), such as New Year's Day, the birthday of Martin Luther King, Jr., Washington's Birthday, Memorial Day, Independence Day, Labor Day, Columbus Day, Veterans Day, Thanksgiving Day, and Christmas Day.

(7) Card issuer means a person that issues a credit card or that person's agent with respect to the card.

(8) Cardholder means a natural person to whom a credit card is issued for consumer credit purposes, or a natural person who has agreed with the card issuer to pay consumer credit obligations arising from the

issuance of a credit card to another natural person. For purposes of § 226.12(a) and (b), the term includes any person to whom a credit card is issued for any purpose, including business, commercial, or agricultural use, or a person who

{{12-31-01 p.6644}} has agreed with the card issuer to pay obligations arising from the issuance of such a credit card to another person.

(9) Cash price means the price at which a creditor, in the ordinary course of business, offers to sell for cash the property or service that is the subject of the transaction. At the creditor's option, the term may include the price of accessories, services related to the sale, service contracts and taxes and fees for license, title, and registration. The term does not include any finance charge.

(10) Closed-end credit means consumer credit other than "open-end credit" as defined in this section.

(11) Consumer means a cardholder or a natural person to whom consumer credit is offered or extended. However, for purposes of rescission under §§ 226.15 and 226.23, the term also includes a natural person in whose principal dwelling a security interest is or will be retained or acquired, if that person's ownership interest in the dwelling is or will be subject to the security interest.

(12) Consumer credit means credit offered or extended to a consumer primarily for personal, family, or household purposes.

(13) Consummation means the time that a consumer becomes contractually obligated on a credit transaction.

(14) Credit means the right to defer payment of debt or to incur debt and defer its payment.

(15) Credit card means any card, plate, coupon book, or other single credit device that may be used from time to time to obtain credit. "Charge card" means a credit card on an account for which no periodic rate is used to compute a finance charge.

(16) Credit sale means a sale in which the seller is a creditor. The term includes a bailment or lease (unless terminable without penalty at any

time by the consumer) under which the consumer:

(i) Agrees to pay as compensation for use a sum substantially equivalent to, or in excess of, the total value of the property and services involved; and

(ii) Will become (or has the option to become), for no additional consideration or for nominal consideration, the owner of the property upon compliance with the agreement.

(17) Creditor means:

(i) A person (A) who regularly extends consumer credit[3] that is subject to a finance charge or is payable by written agreement in more than four installments (not including a downpayment), and (B) to whom the obligation is initially payable, either on the face of the note or contract, or by agreement when there is no note or contract.

(ii) For purposes of §§ 226.4(c)(8) (discounts), 226.9(d) (Finance charge imposed at time of transaction), and 226.12(e) (Prompt notification of returns and crediting of refunds), a person that honors a credit card.

(iii) For purposes of subpart B, any card issuer that extends either open-end credit or credit that is not subject to a finance charge and is not payable by written agreement in more than four installments.

(iv) For purposes of subpart B (except for the credit and charge card disclosures contained in §§ 226.5a and 226.9(e) and (f), the finance charge disclosures contained in §§ 226.6(a) and 226.7(d) through (g) and the right of rescission set forth in § 226.15) and subpart C, any card issuer that extends closed-end credit that is subject to a finance charge or is payable by written agreement in more than four installments.

(18) Downpayment means an amount, including the value of any property used as a trade-in, paid to a seller to reduce the cash price of goods or services purchased in a credit

{{4-30-04 p.6645}}sale transaction. A deferred portion of a downpayment may be treated as part of the downpayment if it is payable not later than the due date of the second otherwise regularly scheduled payment and is not subject to a finance charge.

(19) Dwelling means a residential structure that contains one to four units, whether or not that structure is attached to real property. The term includes an individual condominium unit, cooperative unit, mobile home, and trailer, if it is used as a residence.

(20) Open-end credit means consumer credit extended by a creditor under a plan in which:

(i) The creditor reasonably contemplates repeated transactions;

(ii) The creditor may impose a finance charge from time to time on an outstanding unpaid balance; and

(iii) The amount of credit that may be extended to the consumer during the term of the plan (up to any limit set by the creditor) is generally made available to the extent that any outstanding balance is repaid.

(21) Periodic rate means a rate of finance charge that is or may be imposed by a creditor on a balance for a day, week, month, or other subdivision of a year.

(22) Person means a natural person or an organization, including a corporation, partnership, proprietorship, association, cooperative, estate, trust, or government unit.

(23) Prepaid finance charge means any finance charge paid separately in cash or by check before or at consummation of a transaction, or withheld from the proceeds of the credit at any time.

(24) Residential mortgage transaction means a transaction in which a mortgage, deed of trust, purchase money security interest arising under an installment sales contract, or equivalent consensual security interest is created or retained in the consumer's principal dwelling to finance the acquisition or initial construction of that dwelling.

(25) Security interest means an interest in property that secures performance of a consumer credit obligation and that is recognized by state or federal law. It does not include incidental interests such as interests in proceeds, accessions, additions, fixtures, insurance proceeds (whether or not the creditor is a loss payee or beneficiary),

premium rebates, or interests in after-acquired property. For purposes of disclosure under §§ 226.6 and 226.18, the term does not include an interest that arises solely by operation of law. However, for purposes of the right of rescission under §§ 226.15 and 226.23, the term does include interests that arise solely by operation of law.

(26) State means any state, the District of Columbia, the Commonwealth of Puerto Rico, and any territory or possession of the United States.

(b) Rules of construction. For purposes of this regulation, the following rules of construction apply:

(1) Where appropriate, the singular form of a word includes the plural form and plural includes singular.

(2) Where the words "obligation" and "transaction" are used in this regulation, they refer to a consumer credit obligation or transaction, depending upon the context. Where the word "credit" is used in this regulation, it means "consumer credit" unless the context clearly indicates otherwise.

(3) Unless defined in this regulation, the words used have the meanings given to them by state law or contract.

(4) Footnotes have the same legal effect as the text of the regulation.

(5) Where the word "amount" is used in this regulation to describe disclosure requirements, it refers to a numerical amount.

[Codified to 12 C.F.R. § 226.2]

[Section 226.2 amended at 46 Fed. Reg. 29246, June 1, 1981; 47 Fed. Reg. 7392, February 19, 1982; 48 Fed. Reg. 14886, April 6, 1983, effective October 1, 1982; 54 Fed. Reg. 13865, April 6, 1989, effective April 3, 1989, but compliance is optional until August 31, 1989; 60 Fed. Reg. 15471, March 24, 1995, effective March 22, 1995, compliance is optional until October 1, 1995; 61 Fed. Reg. 49245, September 19, 1996, effective October 21, 1996; 69 Fed. Reg. 16773, March 31, 2004]

{{4-30-04 p.6646}}

§ 226.3 Exempt transactions.

This regulation does not apply to the following:

(a) Business, commercial, agricultural, or organizational credit. [4]

(1) An extension of credit primarily for a business, commercial or agricultural purpose.

(2) An extension of credit to other than a natural person, including credit to government agencies or instrumentalities.

(b) Credit over $25,000 not secured by real property or a dwelling. An extension of credit not secured by real property, or by personal property used or expected to be used as the principal dwelling of the consumer, in which the amount financed exceeds $25,000 or in which there is an express written commitment to extend credit in excess of $25,000.

(c) Public utility credit. An extension of credit that involves public utility services provided through pipe, wire, other connected facilities, or radio or similar transmission (including extensions of such facilities), if the charges for service, delayed payment, or any discounts for prompt payment are filed with or regulated by any government unit. The financing of durable goods or home improvements by a public utility is not exempt.

(d) Securities or commodities accounts. Transactions in securities or commodities accounts in which credit is extended by a broker-dealer registered with the Securities and Exchange Commission or the Commodity Futures Trading Commission.

(e) Home fuel budget plans. An installment agreement for the purchase of home fuels in which no finance charge is imposed.

(f) Student loan programs. Loans made, insured, or guaranteed pursuant to a program authorized by title IV of the Higher Education Act of 1965 (20 U.S.C. 1070 et seq.).

[Codified to 12 C.F.R. § 226.3]

[Section 226.3 amended at 48 Fed. Reg. 14886, April 6, 1983, effective October 1, 1982]

§ 226.4 Finance charge.

(a) Definition. The finance charge is the cost of consumer credit as a dollar amount. It includes any charge payable directly or indirectly by the consumer and imposed directly or indirectly by the creditor as an incident to or a condition of the extension of credit. It does not include any charge of a type payable in a comparable cash transaction.

(1) Charges by third parties. The finance charge includes fees and amounts charged by someone other than the creditor, unless otherwise excluded under this section, if the creditor:

(i) requires the use of a third party as a condition of or an incident to the extension of credit, even if the consumer can choose the third party; or

(ii) retains a portion of the third-party charge, to the extent of the portion retained.

(2) Special rule; closing agent charges. Fees charged by a third party that conducts the loan closing (such as a settlement agent, attorney, or escrow or title company) are finance charges only if the creditor:

(i) Requires the particular services for which the consumer is charged;

(ii) Requires the imposition of the charge; or

(iii) Retains a portion of the third-party charge, to the extent of the portion retained.

(3) Special rule; mortgage broker fees. Fees charged by a mortgage broker (including fees paid by the consumer directly to the broker or to the creditor for delivery to the broker) are finance charges even if the creditor does not require the consumer to use a mortgage broker

and even if the creditor does not retain any portion of the charge.

(b) Example of finance charge. The finance charge includes the following types of charges, except for charges specifically excluded by paragraphs (c) through (e) of this section:

{{10-31-96 p.6647}}

(1) Interest, time price differential, and any amount payable under an add-on or discount system of additional charges.

(2) Service, transaction, activity, and carrying charges, including any charge imposed on a checking or other transaction account to the extent that the charge exceeds the charge for a similar account without a credit feature.

(3) Points, loan fees, assumption fees, finder's fees, and similar charges.

(4) Appraisal, investigation, and credit report fees.

(5) Premiums or other charges for any guarantee or insurance protecting the creditor against the consumer's default or other credit loss.

(6) Charges imposed on a creditor by another person for purchasing or accepting a consumer's obligation, if the consumer is required to pay the charges in cash, as an addition to the obligation, or as a deduction from the proceeds of the obligation.

(7) Premiums or other charges for credit life, accident, health, or loss-of-income insurance, written in connection with a credit transaction.

(8) Premiums or other charges for insurance against loss of or damage to property, or against liability arising out of the ownership or use of property, written in connection with a credit transaction.

(9) Discounts for the purpose of inducing payment by a means other than the use of credit.

(10) Debt cancellation fees. Charges or premiums paid for debt cancellation coverage written in connection with a credit transaction, whether or not the debt cancellation coverage is insurance under applicable law.

(c) Charges excluded from the finance charge. The following charges are not finance charges:

(1) Application fees charged to all applicants for credit, whether or not credit is actually extended.

(2) Charges for actual unanticipated late payment, for exceeding a credit limit or for delinquency, default, or a similar occurrence.

(3) Charges imposed by a financial institution for paying items that overdraw an account, unless the payment of such items and the imposition of the charge were previously agreed upon in writing.

(4) Fees charged for participation in a credit plan, whether assessed on an annual or other periodic basis.

(5) Seller's points.

(6) Interest forfeited as a result of an interest reduction required by law on a time deposit used as security for an extension of credit.

(7) Real-estate related fees. The following fees in a transaction secured by real property or in a residential mortgage transaction, if the fees are bona fide and reasonable in amount:

(i) Fees for title examination, abstract of title, title insurance, property survey, and similar purposes.

(ii) Fees for preparing loan-related documents, such as deeds, mortgages, and reconveyance or settlement documents.

(iii) Notary, and credit report fees.

(iv) Property appraisal fees or fees for inspections to assess the value or condition of the property if the service is performed prior to closing, including fees related to pest infestation or flood hazard determinations.

(v) Amounts required to be paid into escrow or trustee accounts if the amounts would not otherwise be included in the finance charge.

(8) Discounts offered to induce payment for a purchase by cash, check, or other means, as provided in § 167(b) of the act.

(d) Insurance and debt cancellation coverage. (1) Voluntary credit. Premiums for credit life, accident, health, or loss-of-income insurance may be excluded from the finance charge if the following conditions are met:

{{10-31-96 p.6648}}

(i) The insurance coverage is not required by the creditor, and this fact is disclosed in writing.

(ii) The premium for the initial term of insurance coverage is disclosed. If the term of insurance is less than the term of the transaction, the term of insurance also shall be disclosed. The premium may be disclosed on a unit-cost basis only in open-end credit transactions, closed-end credit transactions by mail or telephone under § 226.17(g), and certain closed-end credit transactions involving an insurance plan that limits the total amount of indebtedness subject to coverage.

(iii) The consumer signs or initials an affirmative written request for the insurance after receiving the disclosures specified in this paragraph. Any consumer in the transaction may sign or initial the request.

(2) Premiums for insurance against loss of or damage to property, or against liability arising out of the ownership or use of property, [5] may be excluded from the finance charge if the following conditions are met:

(i) The insurance coverage may be obtained from a person of the consumer's choice, [6] and this fact is disclosed.

(ii) If the coverage is obtained from or through the creditor, the premium for the initial term of insurance coverage shall be disclosed. If the term of insurance is less than the term of the transaction, the term of insurance shall also be disclosed. The premium may be disclosed on a unit-cost basis only in open-end credit transactions, closed-end credit transactions by mail or telephone under § 226.17(g), and certain closed-end credit transactions involving an insurance plan that limits the total amount of indebtedness subject to coverage.

(3) Voluntary debt cancellation fees. (i) Charges or premiums paid for debt cancellation coverage of the type specified in paragraph (d)(3)(ii) of this section may be excluded from the finance charge, whether or not the coverage is insurance, if the following conditions are met:

(A) The debt cancellation agreement or coverage is not required by the creditor, and this fact is disclosed in writing;

(B) The fee or premium for the initial term of coverage is disclosed. If the term of coverage is less than the term of the credit transaction, the term of coverage also shall be disclosed. The fee or premium may be disclosed on a unit-cost basis only in open-end credit transactions, closed-end credit transactions by mail or telephone under § 226.17(g), and certain closed-end credit transactions involving a debt cancellation agreement that limits the total amount of indebtedness subject to coverage;

(C) The consumer signs or initials an affirmative written request for coverage after receiving the disclosures specified in this paragraph. Any consumer in the transaction may sign or initial the request.

(ii) Paragraph (d)(3)(i) of this section applies to fees paid for debt cancellation coverage that provides for cancellation of all or part of the debtor's liability for amounts exceeding the value of the collateral securing the obligation, or in the event of the loss of life, health, or income or in case of accident.

(e) Certain security interest charges. If itemized and disclosed, the following charges may be excluded from the finance charge:

(1) Taxes and fees prescribed by law that actually are or will be paid to public officials for determining the existence of or for perfecting, releasing, or satisfying a security interest.

(2) The premium for insurance in lieu of perfecting a security interest to the extent that the premium does not exceed the fees described in paragraph (e)(1) of this section that otherwise would be payable.
{{8-31-01 p.6648.01}}

(3) Taxes on security instruments. Any tax levied on security instruments or on documents evidencing indebtedness if the payment of such taxes is a requirement for recording the instrument securing the evidence of indebtedness.

(f) Prohibited offsets. Interest, dividends, or other income received or to be received by the consumer on deposits or investments shall not be deducted in computing the finance charge.

[Codified to 12 C.F.R. § 226.4]

[Section 226.4 amended at 61 Fed. Reg. 49245, September 19, 1996, effective October 21, 1996]

[1] The meaning of "regularly" is explained in the definition of "creditor" in § 226.2(a)....

[2] [Reserved] ....

[3] A person regularly extends consumer credit only if it extended credit (other than credit subject to the requirements of § 226.32) more than 25 times (or more than five times for transactions secured by a dwelling) in the preceding calendar year. If a person did not meet these numerical standards in the preceding calendar year, the numerical standards shall be applied to the current calendar year. A person regularly extends consumer credit if, in any 12-month period, the person originates more than one credit extension that is subject to the requirements of § 226.32 or one or more such credit extensions through a mortgage broker.

[4] The provisions in § 226.12(a) and (b) governing the issurance of credit cards and the liability for their unauthorized use apply to all credit cards, even if the credit cards are issued for use in connection with extensions of credit that otherwise are exempt under this section....

[5] This includes single interest insurance if the insurer waives all right of subrogation against the consumer....

[6] A creditor may reserve the right to refuse to accept, for

reasonable cause, an insurer offered by the consumer....|

Subpart E—Special Rules for Certain Home Mortgage Transactions (from www.fdic.gov)

§ 226.31 General rules.

(a) Relation to other subparts in this part. The requirements and limitations of this subpart are in addition to and not in lieu of those contained in other subparts of this part.

(b) Form of disclosures. (1) General. The creditor shall make the disclosures required by this subpart clearly and conspicuously in writing, in a form that the consumer may keep.

(2) Electronic communication. For rules governing the electronic delivery of disclosures, including a definition of electronic communication, see § 226.36.

(c) Timing of disclosure--(1) Disclosures for certain closed-end home mortgages. The creditor shall furnish the disclosures required by § 226.32 at least three business days prior to consummation of a mortgage transaction covered by § 226.32.

(i) Change in terms. After complying with paragraph (c)(1) of this section and prior to consummation, if the creditor changes any term that makes the disclosures inaccurate, new disclosures shall be provided in accordance with the requirements of this subpart.

(ii) Telephone disclosures. A creditor may provide new disclosures by telephone if the consumer initiates the change and if, at consummation:

(A) The creditor provides new written disclosures; and

(B) The consumer and creditor sign a statement that the new disclosures were provided by telephone at least three days prior to consummation.

(iii) Consumer's waiver of waiting period before consummation. The consumer may, after receiving the disclosures required by paragraph (c)(1) of this section, modify or waive the three-day waiting period between delivery of those disclosures and consummation if the consumer determines that the extension of credit is needed to meet a bona fide personal financial emergency. To modify or waive the right, the consumer shall give the creditor a dated written statement that describes the emergency, specifically modifies or waives the waiting period, and bears the signature of all the consumers entitled to the waiting period. Printed forms for this purpose are prohibited, except when creditors are permitted to use printed forms pursuant to § 226.23(e)(2).

(2) Disclosures for reverse mortgages. The creditor shall furnish the disclosures required by § 226.33 at least three business days prior to:

(i) Consummation of a closed-end credit transaction; or

(ii) The first transaction under an open-end credit plan.

(d) Basis of disclosures and use of estimates.--(1) Legal Obligation. Disclosures shall reflect the terms of the legal obligation between the parties.

(2) Estimates. If any information necessary for an accurate disclosure is unknown to the creditor, the creditor shall make the disclosure based on the best information reasonably

{{12-31-01 p.6670.01}}available at the time the disclosure is provided, and shall state clearly that the disclosure is an estimate.

(3) Pre-diem interest. For a transaction in which a portion of the interest is determined on a per-diem basis and collected at consummation, any disclosure affected by the per-diem interest shall be considered accurate if the disclosure is based on the information known to the creditor at the time that the disclosure documents are prepared.

(e) Multiple creditors; multiple consumers. If a transaction involves more than one creditor, only one set of disclosures shall be given and the creditors shall agree among themselves which creditor must comply with the requirements that this part imposes on any or all of them. If there is more than one consumer, the disclosures may be made to any consumer who is primarily liable on the obligation. If the transaction is rescindable under § 226.15 or § 226.23, however, the disclosures shall be made to each consumer who has the right to rescind.

(f) Effect of subsequent events. If a disclosure becomes inaccurate because of an event that occurs after the creditor delivers the required disclosures, the inaccuracy is not a violation of Regulation Z (12 CFR part 226), although new disclosures may be required for mortgages covered by § 226.32 under paragraph (c) of this section, § 226.9(c), § 226.19, or § 226.20.

(g) Accuracy of annual percentage rate. For purposes of § 226.32, the annual percentage rate shall be considered accurate, and may be used in determining whether a transaction is covered by § 226.32, if it is accurate according to the requirements and within the tolerances under § 226.22. The finance charge tolerances for rescission under § 226.23(g) or (h) shall not apply for this purpose.

[Codified to 12 C.F.R. § 226.31]

[Section 226.31 added at 60 Fed. Reg. 15471, March 24, 1995, effective March 22, 1995, but compliance is optional until October 1, 1995; 61 Fed. Reg. 49247, September 19, 1996, effective October 21, 1996; amended at 66 Fed. Reg. 17339, March 30, 2001, effective March 30, 2001]

§ 226.32 Requirements for certain closed-end home mortgages.

(a) Coverage. (1) Except as provided in paragraph (a)(2) of this section, the requirements of this section apply to a consumer credit transaction that is secured by the consumer's principal dwelling, and in which either:

(i) The annual percentage rate at consummation will exceed by more than 8 percentage points for first-lien loans, or by more than 10 percentage points for subordinate-lien loans, the yield on Treasury securities having comparable periods of maturity to the loan maturity as of the fifteenth day of the month immediately preceding the month in which the application for the extension of credit is received by the creditor; or

(ii) The total points and fees payable by the consumer at or before loan closing will exceed the greater of 8 percent of the total loan amount, or $400; the $400 figure shall be adjusted annually on January 1 by the annual percentage change in the Consumer Price Index that was reported on the preceding June 1.

(2) This section does not apply to the following:

(i) A residential mortgage transaction.

(ii) A reverse mortgage transaction subject to § 226.33.

(iii) An open-end credit plan subject to subpart B of this part.

(b) Definitions. For purposes of this subpart, the following definitions apply:

(1) For purposes of paragraph (a)(1)(ii) of this section, points and fees mean:

(i) All items required to be disclosed under § 226.4(a) and 226.4(b), except interest or the time-price differential;

(ii) All compensation paid to mortgage brokers; and

(iii) All items listed in § 226.4(c)(7) (other than amounts held for future payment of taxes) unless the charge is reasonable, the creditor receives no direct or indirect

{{12-31-01 p.6670.02}}compensation in connection with the charge, and the charge is not paid to an affiliate of the creditor; and

(iv) Premiums or other charges for credit life, accident, health, or loss-of-income insurance, or debt-cancellation coverage (whether or not the debt-cancellation coverage is insurance under applicable law) that provides for cancellation of all or part of the consumer's liability in the event of the loss of life, health, or income or in the case of accident, written in connection with the credit transaction.

(2) Affiliate means any company that controls, is controlled by, or is under common control with another company, as set forth in the Bank Holding Company Act of 1956 (12 U.S.C. 1841 et seq.)

(c) Disclosures. In addition to other disclosures required by this part, in a mortgage subject to this section, the creditor shall disclose the following in conspicuous type size:

(1) Notices. The following statement: "You are not required to complete this agreement merely because you have received these disclosures or have signed a loan application. If you obtain this loan, the lender will have a mortgage on your home. You could lose your home, and any money you have put into it, if you do no meet your obligations under the loan."

(2) Annual percentage rate. The annual percentage rate.

(3) Regular payment; balloon payment. The amount of the regular monthly (or other periodic) payment and the amount of any balloon payment. The regular payment disclosed under this paragraph shall be treated as accurate if it is based on an amount borrowed that is deemed accurate and is disclosed under paragraph (c)(5) of this section.

(4) Variable-rate. For variable-rate transactions, a statement that the interest rate and monthly payment may increase, and the amount of the single maximum monthly payment, based on the maximum interest rate required to be disclosed under § 226.30.

(5) Amount borrowed. For a mortgage refinancing, the total amount the consumer will borrow, as reflected by the face amount of the note; and where the amount borrowed includes premiums or other charges for optional credit insurance or debt-cancellation coverage, that fact shall be stated, grouped together with the disclosure of the amount borrowed. The disclosure of the amount borrowed shall be treated as accurate if it is not more than $100 above or below the amount required to be disclosed.

(d) Limitations. A mortgage transaction subject to this section shall not include the following terms:

(1)(i) Balloon payment. For a loan with a term of less than five years, a payment schedule with regular periodic payments that when aggregated do not fully amortize the outstanding principal balance.

(ii) Exception. The limitations in paragraph (d)(1)(i) of this section do not apply to loans with maturities of less than one year, if the purpose of the loan is a "bridge" loan connected with the acquisition or construction of a dwelling intended to become the consumer's principal dwelling.

(2) Negative amortization. A payment schedule with regular periodic payments that cause the principal balance to increase.

(3) Advance payments. A payment schedule that consolidates more than two periodic payments and pays them in advance from the proceeds.

(4) Increased interest rate. An increase in the interest rate after default.

(5) Rebates. A refund calculated by a method less favorable than the actuarial method (as defined by section 933(d) of the Housing and Community Development Act of 1992, 15 U.S.C. 1615(d)), for rebates of interest arising from a loan acceleration due to default.

(6) Prepayment penalties. Except as allowed under paragraph (d)(7) of this section, a penalty for paying all or part of the principal before the date on which the principal is due. A prepayment penalty includes computing a refund of unearned interest by a method that is less favorable to the consumer than the actuarial method, as defined by section 933(d) of the Housing and Community Development Act of 1992.

{{2-28-02 p.6670.02-A}}

(7) Prepayment penalty exception. A mortgage transaction subject to this section may provide for a prepayment penalty otherwise permitted by law (including a refund calculated according to the rule of 78s) if:

(i) The penalty can be exercised only for the first five years following consummation;

(ii) The source of the prepayment funds is not a refinancing by the creditor or an affiliate of the creditor; and

(iii) At consummation, the consumer's total monthly debts (including amounts owed under the mortgage) do not exceed 50 percent of the consumer's monthly gross income, as verified by the consumer's signed financial statement, a credit report, and payment records for employment income.

(8) Due-on-demand clause. A demand feature that permits the creditor to terminate the loan in advance of the original maturity date and to demand repayment of the entire outstanding balance, except in the following circumstances:

(i) There is fraud or material misrepresentation by the consumer in connection with the loan;

(ii) The consumer fails to meet the repayment terms of the agreement for any outstanding balance; or

(iii) There is any action or inaction by the consumer that adversely affects the creditor's security for the loan, or any right of the creditor in such security.

[Codified to 12 C.F.R. § 226.32]

[Section 226.32 added at 60 Fed. Reg. 15472, March 24, 1995, effective March 22, 1995, but compliance is optional until October 1, 1995; as amended at 66 Fed. Reg. 65617, December 20, 2001, effective December 20, 2001, but compliance mandatory as of October 1, 2002]

§ 226.33 Requirements for reverse mortgages.

(a) Definition. For purposes of this subpart, reverse mortgage transaction means a nonrecourse consumer credit obligation in which:

(1) A mortgage, deed of trust, or equivalent consensual security interest securing one or more advances is created in the consumer's

principal dwelling; and

(2) Any principal, interest, or shared appreciation or equity is due and payable (other than in the case of default) only after:

(i) The consumer dies;

(ii) The dwelling is transferred; or

(iii) The consumer ceases to occupy the dwelling as a principal dwelling.

(b) Content of disclosures. In addition to other disclosures required by this part, in a reverse mortgage transaction the creditor shall provide the following disclosures in a form substantially similar to the model form found in paragraph (d) of Appendix K of this part:

(1) Notice. A statement that the consumer is not obligated to complete the reverse mortgage transaction merely because the consumer has received the disclosures required by this section or has signed an application for a reverse mortgage loan.

(2) Total annual loan cost rates. A good-faith projection of the total cost of the credit, determined in accordance with paragraph (c) of this section and expressed as a table of "total annual loan cost rates," using that term, in accordance with Appendix K of this part.

(3) Itemization of pertinent information. An itemization of loan terms, charges, the age of the youngest borrower and the appraised property value.

(4) Explanation of table. An explanation of the table of total annual loan cost rates as provided in the model form found in paragraph (d) of Appendix K of this part.

(c) Projected total cost of credit. The projected total cost of credit shall reflect the following factors, as applicable:

(1) Costs to consumer. All costs and charges to the consumer, including the costs of any annuity the consumer purchases as part of the reverse mortgage transaction.

{{2-28-02 p.6670.02-B}}

(2) Payments to consumer. All advances to and for the benefit of the

consumer, including annuity payments that the consumer will receive from an annuity that the consumer purchases as part of the reverse mortgage transaction.

(3) Additional creditor compensation. Any shared appreciation or equity in the dwelling that the creditor is entitled by contract to receive.

(4) Limitations on consumer liability. Any limitation on the consumer's liability (such as nonrecourse limits and equity conservation agreements).

(5) Assumed annual appreciation rates. Each of the following assumed annual appreciation rates for the dwelling:

(i) 0 percent.

(ii) 4 percent.

(iii) 8 percent.

(6) Assumed loan period. (i) Each of the following assumed loan periods, as provided in Appendix L of this part:

(A) Two years.

(B) The actuarial life expectancy of the consumer to become obligated on the reverse mortgage transaction (as of that consumer's most recent birthday). In the case of multiple consumers, the period shall be the actuarial life expectancy of the youngest consumer (as of that consumer's most recent birthday).

(C) The actuarial life expectancy specified by paragraph (c)(6)(i)(B) of this section, multiplied by a factor of 1.4 and rounded to the nearest full year.

(ii) At the creditor's option, the actuarial life expectancy specified by paragraph (c)(6)(i)(B) of this section, multiplied by a factor of .5 and rounded to the nearest full year.

[Codified to 12 C.F.R. § 226.33]

[Section 226.33 added at 60 Fed. Reg. 15473, March 24, 1995, effective March 22, 1995, but compliance is optional until October 1, 1995]

§ 226.34 Prohibited acts or practices in connection with credit secured by a consumer's dwelling.

(a) Prohibited acts or practices for loans subject to § 226.32. A creditor extending mortgage credit subject to § 226.32 shall not--
(1) Home improvement contracts. Pay a contractor under a home improvement contract from the proceeds of a mortgage covered by § 226.32, other than:
(i) By an instrument payable to the consumer or jointly to the consumer and the contractor; or
(ii) At the election of the consumer, through a third-party escrow agent in accordance with terms established in a written agreement signed by the consumer, the creditor, and the contractor prior to the disbursement.
(2) Notice to assignee. Sell or otherwise assign a mortgage subject to § 226.32 without furnishing the following statement to the purchaser or assignee: "Notice: This is a mortgage subject to special rules under the federal Truth in Lending Act. Purchasers or assignees of this mortgage could be liable for all claims and defenses with respect to the mortgage that the borrower could assert against the creditor."
(3) Refinancings within one-year period. Within one year of having extended credit subject to § 226.32, refinance any loan subject to § 226.32 to the same borrower into another loan subject to § 226.32, unless the refinancing is in the borrower's interest. An assignee holding or servicing an extension of mortgage credit subject to § 226.32, shall not, for the remainder of the one-year period following the date of origination of the credit, refinance any loan subject to § 226.32 to the same borrower into another loan subject to § 226.32, unless the refinancing is in the borrower's interest. A creditor (or assignee) is

prohibited from engaging in acts or practices to evade this provision, including a pattern or practice of arranging for the refinancing of its own loans by affiliated or unaffiliated creditors, or modifying a loan agreement (whether or not the existing loan is satisfied and replaced by the new loan) and charging a fee.

{{2-28-02 p.6670.03}}

(4) Repayment ability. Engage in a pattern or practice of extending credit subject to § 226.32 to a consumer based on the consumer's collateral without regard to the consumer's repayment ability, including the consumer's current and expected income, current obligations, and employment. There is a presumption that a creditor has violated this paragraph (a)(4) if the creditor engages in a pattern or practice of making loans subject to § 226.32 without verifying and documenting consumers' repayment ability.(b) Prohibited acts or practices for dwelling-secured loans; open-end credit. In connection with credit secured by the consumer's dwelling that does not meet the definition in § 226.2(a)(20), a creditor shall not structure a home-secured loan as an open-end plan to evade the requirements of § 226.32.

[Codified to 12 C.F.R. § 226.34]

[Section 226.34 added at 66 Fed. Reg. 65618, December 20, 2001, effective December 20, 2001, but compliance mandatory as of October 1, 2002]

§ 226.35 [Reserved]

Subpart F—Electronic Communication

§ 226.36 Requirements for electronic communication.

(a) Definition. "Electronic communication" means a message

transmitted electronically between a creditor and a consumer in a format that allows visual text to be displayed on equipment, for example, a personal computer monitor.

(b) General rule. In accordance with the Electronic Signatures in Global and National Commerce Act (the E-Sign Act) (15 U.S.C. 7001 et seq.) and the rules of this part, a creditor may provide by electronic communication any disclosure required by this part to be in writing.

(c) When consent is required. Under the E-Sign Act, a creditor is required to obtain a consumer's affirmative consent when providing disclosures related to a transaction. For purposes of this requirement, the disclosures required under §§ 226.5a, 226.5b(d) and 226.5b(e), 226.16, 226.17(g)(1) through (5), 226.19(b) and 226.24 are deemed not to be related to a transaction.

(d) Address or location to receive electronic communication. A creditor that uses electronic communication to provide disclosures required by this part shall:

(1) Send the disclosure to the consumer's electronic address; or

(2) Make the disclosure available at another location such as an Internet web site; and

(i) Alert the consumer of the disclosure's availability by sending a notice to the consumer's electronic address (or to a postal address, at the creditor's option). The notice shall identify the account involved and the address of the Internet web site or other location where the disclosure is available; and

(ii) Make the disclosure available for at least 90 days from the date the disclosure first becomes available or from the date of the notice alerting the consumer of the disclosure, whichever comes later.

(3) Exceptions. A creditor need not comply with paragraphs (d)(2)(i) and (ii) of this section for the disclosures required under §§ 226.5a, 226.5b(d) and 226.5b(e), 226.16, 226.17(g)(1) through (5), 226.19(b) and 226.24.

(e) Redelivery. When a disclosure provided by electronic

communication is returned to a creditor undelivered, the creditor shall take reasonable steps to attempt redelivery using information in its files.

(f)   Electronic signatures. An electronic signature as defined under the E-Sign satisfies any requirement under this part for a consumer's signature or initials.

[Codified to 12 C.F.R. § 226.36]

[Section 226.36 added at 66 Fed. Reg. 17339, March 30, 2001, effective March 30, 2001]

[50] Compliance with this section will constitute compliance with the disclosure requirements on limitations on increases in footnote 12 to §§ 226.6(a)(2) and 226.18(f)(2) until October 1, 1988.

APPENDIX 4

HOME MORTGAGE DISCLOSURE ACT OF 1975

AN ACT

To extend the authority for the flexible regulation of interest rates on deposits and share accounts in depository institutions, to extend the National Commission on Electronic Fund Transfers, and to provide for home mortgage disclosure.

Be it enacted by the Senate and House of Representatives of the United States of America in Congress assembled,

* * * * *

TITLE III—HOME MORTGAGE DISCLOSURE

SHORT TITLE

SEC. 301. This title may be cited as the "Home Mortgage Disclosure Act of 1975".

[Codified to 12 U.S.C. 2801 note]

[Source: Section 301 of title III of the Act of December 31, 1975 (Pub. L. No. 94--200; 89 Stat. 1125), effective June 28, 1976]

FINDINGS AND PURPOSES

SEC. 302. (a) The Congress finds that some depository institutions have sometimes contributed to the decline of certain geographic areas by their failure pursuant to their chartering responsibilities to provide adequate home financing to qualified applicants on reasonable terms and conditions.

(b) The purpose of this title is to provide the citizens and public officials of the United States with sufficient information to enable them to determine whether depository institutions are filling their obligations to serve the housing needs of the communities and neighborhoods in which they are located and to assist public officials in their determination of the distribution of public sector investments in a manner designed to improve the private investment environment.

(c) Nothing in this title is intended to, nor shall it be construed to, encourage unsound lending practices or the allocation of credit.

[Codified to 12 U.S.C. 2801]

[Source: Section 302 of title III of the Act of December 31, 1975 (Pub. L. No. 94--200; 89 Stat. 1125), effective June 28, 1976]

DEFINITIONS

SEC. 303. For the purposes of this title--

(1) the term "mortgage loan" means a loan which is secured by residential real property or a home improvement loan;

(2) the term "depository institution"--

(A) means--

(i) any bank (as defined in section 3(a)(1) of the Federal Deposit Insurance Act);

(ii) any savings association (as defined in section 3(b)(1) of the Federal

Deposit Insurance Act); and

(iii) any credit union,

which makes federally related mortgage loans as determined by the Board; and

(B) includes any other lending institution (as defined in paragraph (4)) other than any institution described in subparagraph (A);

(3) the term "completed application" means an application in which the creditor has received the information that is regularly obtained in evaluating applications for the amount and type of credit requested; {{4-28-00 p.7302}}

(4) the term "other lending institutions" means any person engaged for profit in the business of mortgage lending;

(5) the term "Board" means the Board of Governors of the Federal Reserve System; and

(6) the term "Secretary" means the Secretary of Housing and Urban Development.

[Codified to 12 U.S.C. 2802]

[Source: Section 303 of title III of the Act of December 31, 1975 (Pub. L. No. 94--200; 89 Stat. 1125), effective June 28, 1976; as amended by section 565(a)(1) of title V of the Act of February 5, 1988 (Pub. L. No. 100--242; 101 Stat. 1945), effective February 5, 1988; section 1211(d) and (e) of title XII of the Act of August 9, 1989 (Pub. L. No. 101--73; 103 Stat. 525), effective August 9, 1989]

MAINTENANCE OF RECORDS AND PUBLIC DISCLOSURE

SEC. 304. (a)(1) Each depository institution which has a home office or branch office located within a primary metropolitan statistical area, metropolitan statistical area, or consolidated metropolitan statistical area that is not comprised of designated primary metropolitan statistical areas, as defined by the Department of Commerce shall compile and make available, in accordance with regulations of the Board, to the public for inspection and copying at the home office, and at least one branch office within each primary metropolitan statistical area, metropolitan statistical area, or consolidated metropolitan statistical area that is not comprised of designated primary metropolitan statistical areas, in which the depository institution has an office the number and total dollar amount of mortgage loans which were (A) originated (or for which the institution received completed applications), or (B) purchased by that institution during each fiscal year (beginning with the last full fiscal year of that institution which immediately preceded the effective date of this title).

(2) The information required to be maintained and made available under paragraph (1) shall also be itemized in order to clearly and conspicuously disclose the following:

(A) The number and dollar amount for each item referred to in paragraph (1), by census tracts, for mortgage loans secured by property located within any county with a population of more than 30,000, within that primary metropolitan statistical area, metropolitan statistical area, or consolidated metropolitan statistical area that is not comprised of designated primary metropolitan statistical areas, otherwise, by county, for mortgage loans secured by property located within any other county within that primary metropolitan statistical area, metropolitan statistical area, or consolidated metropolitan statistical area that is not comprised of designated primary metropolitan statistical areas.

(B) The number and dollar amount for each item referred to in paragraph (1) for all such mortgage loans which are secured by property located outside that primary metropolitan statistical area, metropolitan statistical area, or consolidated metropolitan statistical area that is not comprised of designated primary metropolitan statistical areas.

For the purpose of this paragraph, a depository institution which maintains offices in more than one primary metropolitan statistical area, metropolitan statistical area, or consolidated metropolitan statistical area that is not comprised of designated primary metropolitan statistical areas, shall be required to make the information required by this paragraph available at any such office only to the extent that such information relates to mortgage loans which were originated or purchased (or for which completed applications are received) by an office of that depository institution located in the primary metropolitan statistical area, metropolitan statistical area, or consolidated metropolitan statistical area that is not comprised of designated primary metropolitan statistical areas, in which the office making such information available is located. For purposes of this paragraph, other lending institutions shall be deemed to have a home office or branch office within a primary metropolitan statistical area, metropolitan statistical area, or consolidated metropolitan statistical area that is not comprised of designated primary metropolitan

{{4-28-00 p.7303}} statistical areas if such institutions have originated or purchased or received completed applications for at least 5 mortgage loans in such area in the preceding calendar year.

(b) Any item of information relating to mortgage loans required to be maintained under subsection (a) shall be further itemized in order to disclose for each such item--

(1) the number and dollar amount of mortgage loans which are insured under title II of the National Housing Act or under title V of the Housing Act of 1949 or which are guaranteed under chapter 37 of title 38, United States Code;

(2) the number and dollar amount of mortgage loans made to mortgagors who did not, at the time of execution of the mortgage, intend to reside in the property securing the mortgage loan;

(3) the number and dollar amount of home improvement loans; and

(4) the number and dollar amount of mortgage loans and completed applications involving mortgagors or mortgage applicants grouped

according to census tract, income level, racial characteristics, and gender.

(c) Any information required to be compiled and made available under this section shall be maintained and made available for a period of five years after the close of the first year during which such information is required to be maintained and made available.

(d) Notwithstanding the provisions of subsection (a)(1), data required to be disclosed under this section for 1980 and thereafter shall be disclosed for each calendar year. Any depository institution which is required to make disclosures under this section but which has been making disclosures on some basis other than a calendar year basis shall make available a separate disclosure statement containing data for any period prior to calendar year 1980 which is not covered by the last full year report prior to the 1980 calendar year report.

(e) Subject to subsection (h), the Board shall prescribe a standard format for the disclosures required under this section.

(f) The Federal Financial Institutions Examination Council, in consultation with the Secretary, shall implement a system to facilitate access to data required to be disclosed under this section. Such system shall include arrangements for a central depository of data in each primary metropolitan statistical area, metropolitan statistical area, or consolidated metropolitan statistical area that is not comprised of designated primary metropolitan statistical areas. Disclosure statements shall be made available to the public for inspection and copying at such central depository of data for all depository institutions which are required to disclose information under this section (or which are exempted pursuant to section 306(b)) and which have a home office or branch office within such primary metropolitan statistical area, metropolitan statistical area, or consolidated metropolitan statistical area that is not comprised of designated primary metropolitan statistical areas.

(g) The requirements of subsections (a) and (b) shall not apply with respect to mortgage loans that are--

(1) made (or for which completed applications are received) by any mortgage banking subsidiary of a bank holding company or savings and loan holding company or by any savings and loan service corporation that originates or purchases mortgage loans; and

(2) approved (or for which completed applications are received) by the Secretary for insurance under title I or II of the National Housing Act.

(h) SUBMISSION TO AGENCIES.--The data required to be disclosed under subsection (b)(4) shall be submitted to the appropriate agency for each institution reporting under this title. Notwithstanding the requirement of section 304(a)(2)(A) for disclosure by census tract, the Board, in cooperation with other appropriate regulators, including--

(1) the Office of the Comptroller of the Currency for national banks and Federal branches and Federal agencies of foreign banks;

(2) the Director of the Office of Thrift Supervision for savings associations;

(3) the Federal Deposit Insurance Corporation for banks insured by the Federal Deposit Insurance Corporation (other than members of the Federal Reserve System), mutual savings banks, insured State branches of foreign banks, and any other depository {{4-28-00 p.7304}}institution described in section 303(2)(A) which is not otherwise referred to in this paragraph;

(4) the National Credit Union Administration Board for credit unions; and

(5) the Secretary of Housing and Urban Development for other lending institutions not regulated by the agencies referred to in paragraphs (1) through (4),

shall develop regulations prescribing the format for such disclosures, the method for submission of the data to the appropriate regulatory agency, and the procedures for disclosing the information to the public. These regulations shall also require the collection of data required to be disclosed under subsection (b)(4) with respect to loans sold by each institution reporting under this title, and, in addition, shall require disclosure of the class of the purchaser of such loans. Any reporting institution may submit in writing to the appropriate agency such additional data or explanations as it deems relevant to the decision to originate or purchase mortgage loans.

(i) EXEMPTION FROM CERTAIN DISCLOSURE REQUIREMENTS.-- The requirements of subsection (b)(4) shall not apply with respect to any depository institution described in section 303(2)(A) which has total assets, as of the most recent full fiscal year of such institution, of $30,000,000 or less.

(j) LOAN APPLICATION REGISTER INFORMATION.--

(1) IN GENERAL.--

In addition to the information required to be disclosed under subsections (a) and (b) of this section, any depository institution which is required to make disclosures under this section shall make available to the public, upon request, loan application register information (as defined by the Board by regulation) in the form required under regulations prescribed by the Board.

(2) FORMAT OF DISCLOSURE.--

(A) UNEDITED FORMAT.--

Subject to subparagraph (B), the loan application register information described in paragraph (1) may be disclosed by a depository institution without editing or compilation and in the format in which such information is maintained by the institution.

(B) PROTECTION OF APPLICANT'S PRIVACY INTEREST.--

The Board shall require, by regulation, such deletions as the Board may determine to be appropriate to protect--

(i) any privacy interest of any applicant, including the deletion of the applicant's name and identification number, the date of the application, and the date of any determination by the institution with respect to such application; and

(ii) a depository institution from liability under any Federal or State privacy law.

(C) CENSUS TRACT FORMAT ENCOURAGED.--

It is the sense of the Congress that a depository institution should provide loan register information under this section in a format based on the census tract in which the property is located.

(3) CHANGE OF FORM NOT REQUIRED.--

A depository institution meets the disclosure requirement of paragraph (1) if the institution provides the information required under such paragraph in the form in which the institution maintains such information.

(4) REASONABLE CHARGE FOR INFORMATION.--

Any depository institution which provides information under this subsection may impose a reasonable fee for any cost incurred in reproducing such information.

(5) TIME OF DISCLOSURE.--

The disclosure of the loan application register information described in paragraph

(1) for any year pursuant to a request under paragraph (1) shall be made--

(A) in the case of a request made on or before March 1 of the succeeding year, before April 1 of the succeeding year; and

(B) in the case of a request made after March 1 of the succeeding year, before the end of the 30-day period beginning on the date the request is made.

{{4-28-00 p.7305}}

(6) RETENTION OF INFORMATION.--

Notwithstanding subsection (c) of this section, the loan application register information described in paragraph (1) for any year shall be maintained and made available, upon request, for 3 years after the close of the 1st year during which such information is required to be maintained and made available.

(7) MINIMIZING COMPLIANCE COSTS.--

In prescribing regulations under this subsection, the Board shall make every effort to minimize the costs incurred by a depository institution in complying with this subsection and such regulations.

(k) DISCLOSURE OF STATEMENTS BY DEPOSITORY INSTITUTIONS.--

(1) IN GENERAL.--

In accordance with procedures established by the Board pursuant to this section, any depository institution required to make disclosures under this section--

(A) shall make a disclosure statement available, upon request, to the public no later than 3 business days after the institution receives the statement from the Federal Financial Institutions Examination Council; and

(B) may make such statement available on a floppy disc which may be used with a personal computer or in any other media which is not prohibited under regulations prescribed by the Board.

(2) Notice that data is subject to correction after final review.--

Any disclosure statement provided pursuant to paragraph (1) shall be accompanied by a clear and conspicuous notice that the statement is subject to final review and revision, if necessary.

(3) REASONABLE CHARGE FOR INFORMATION.--

Any depository institution which provides a disclosure statement pursuant to paragraph (1) may impose a reasonable fee for any cost incurred in providing or reproducing such statement.

(*l*) Prompt Disclosures.—

(1) IN GENERAL.--

Any disclosure of information pursuant to this section or section 310 shall be made as promptly as possible.

(2) MAXIMUM DISCLOSURE PERIOD.--

(A) 6- AND 9-MONTH MAXIMUM PERIODS.--

Except as provided in subsections (j)(5) and (k)(1) of this section and regulations prescribed by the Board and subject to subparagraph (B), any information required to be disclosed for any year beginning after December 31, 1992, under--

(i) this section shall be made available to the public before September 1 of the succeeding year; and

(ii) section 2809 of this title shall be made available to the public before December 1 of the succeeding year.

(B) SHORTER PERIODS ENCOURAGED AFTER 1994.--

With respect to disclosures of information under this section or section 2809 of this title for any year beginning after December 31, 1993, every effort shall be made--

(i) to make information disclosed under this section available to the public before July 1 of the succeeding year; and

(ii) to make information required to be disclosed under section 2809 of this title available to the public before September 1 of the succeeding year.

(3) IMPROVED PROCEDURE.--

The Federal Financial Institutions Examination Council shall make such changes in the system established pursuant to subsection (f) of this section as may be necessary to carry out the requirements of this subsection.

(m) OPPORTUNITY TO REDUCE COMPLIANCE BURDEN.--

(1) In general.--

(A) SATISFACTION OF PUBLIC AVAILABILITY REUIREMENTS.--A depository institution shall be deemed to have satisfied the public availability requirements of subsection (a)

{{4-28-00 p.7306}} if the institution compiles the information required under that subsection at the home office of the institution and provides notice at the branch locations specified in subsection (a) that such information is available from the home office of the institution upon written request.

(B) Provision of information upon request.--Not later than 15 days after the receipt of a written request for any information required to be compiled under subsection (a), the home office of the depository institution receiving the request shall provide the information pertinent to the location of the branch in question to the person requesting the information.

(2) FORM OF INFORMATION.--In complying with paragraph (1), a depository institution shall, in the sole discretion of the institution, provide the person requesting the information with--

(A) a paper copy of the information requested; or

(B) if acceptable to the person, the information through a form of electronic medium, such as a computer disk.

[Codified to 12 U.S.C. 2803]

[Source: Section 304 of title III of the Act of December 31, 1975 (Pub. L. No. 94--200; 89 Stat. 1125), effective June 28, 1976; as amended by section 340 of title III of the Act of October 8, 1980 (Pub. L. No. 96--399; 94 Stat. 1657--1658), effective October 8, 1980; section 701(a) of title VII of the Act of November 30, 1983 (Pub. L. No. 98--181; 97 Stat. 1266), effective November 30, 1983; sections 565(a)(2) and 570(h) of title V of the Act of February 5, 1988 (Pub. L. No. 100--242; 101 Stat. 1945 and 1950 respectively), effective February 5, 1988; section 1211(a)-(c), (f), (i) and (j) of title XII of the Act of August 9, 1989 (Pub. L. No. 101--73; 103 Stat. 524--526), effective August 9, 1989; section 212(a)(1) of title II of the Act of December 19, 1991 (Pub. L. No. 102--242; 105 Stat. 2299) effective December 19, 1991; section 932(a), (b), of title IX of the Act of October 28, 1992 (Pub. L. No. 102-550; 106 Stat. 3889, and 3891, respectively), effective October 28, 1992; section 2225(b) of title II of the Act of September 30, 1996 (Pub. L. No. 104-208; 110 Stat. 3009-415), effective September 30, 1996]

ENFORCEMENT

SEC. 305. (a) The Board shall prescribe such regulations as may be necessary to carry out the purposes of this title. These regulations may contain such classifications, differentiations, or other provisions, and may provide for such adjustments and exceptions for any class of transactions, as in the judgment of the Board are necessary and proper to effectuate the purposes of this title, and prevent circumvention or evasion thereof, or to facilitate compliance therewith.

(b) Compliance with the requirements imposed under this title shall be enforced under--

(1) section 8 of the Federal Deposit Insurance Act, in the case of--

(A) national banks, and Federal branches and Federal agencies of foreign banks, by the Office of the Comptroller of the Currency;

(B) member banks of the Federal Reserve System (other than national banks), branches and agencies of foreign banks (other than Federal branches, Federal agencies, and insured State branches of foreign banks), commercial lending companies owned or controlled by foreign banks, and organizations operating under section 25 or 25(a) of the Federal Reserve Act, by the Board; and

(C) banks insured by the Federal Deposit Insurance Corporation (other than members of the Federal Reserve System), mutual savings banks as defined in section 3(f) of the Federal Deposit Insurance Act (12 U.S.C. 1813(f)), insured State branches of foreign banks, and any other depository institution not referred to in this paragraph or paragraph (2) or (3) of this subsection, by the Board of Directors of the Federal Deposit Insurance Corporation;

{{4-28-00 p.7307}}

(2) section 8 of the Federal Deposit Insurance Act, by the Director of the Office of Thrift Supervision, in the case of a savings association the deposits of which are insured by the Federal Deposit Insurance Corporation;

(3) the Federal Credit Union Act, by the Administrator of the National Credit Union Administration with respect to any credit union; and

(4) other lending institutions, by the Secretary of Housing and Urban Development.

The terms used in paragraph (1) that are not defined in this title or otherwise defined in section 3(s) of the Federal Deposit Insurance Act (12 U.S.C. 1813(s)) shall have the meaning given to them in section 1(b) of the International Banking Act of 1978 (12 U.S.C. 3101).

(c) For the purpose of the exercise by any agency referred to in subsection (b) of its powers under any Act referred to in that subsection, a violation of any requirement imposed under this title shall be deemed to be a violation of a requirement imposed under that Act. In addition to its powers under any provision of law specifically referred to in subsection (b), each of the agencies referred to in that subsection may exercise, for the purpose of enforcing compliance with any requirement imposed under this title, any other authority conferred on it by law.

[Codified to 12 U.S.C. 2804]

[Source: Section 305 of title III of the Act of December 31, 1975 (Pub. L. No. 94--200; 89 Stat. 1126), effective June 28, 1976; as amended by section 744(p)(1) of title VII and section 1211(g) of title XII of the Act of August 9, 1989 (Pub. L. No. 101--73; 103 Stat. 440), effective August 9, 1989; section 212(a)(2) of title II of the Act of December 19, 1991 (Pub. L. No. 102--242; 105 Stat. 2299), effective December 19, 1991]

RELATION TO STATE LAWS

SEC. 306. (a) This title does not annul, alter, or affect, or exempt any State chartered depository institution subject to the provisions of this title from complying with the laws of any State or subdivision thereof with respect to public disclosure and recordkeeping by depositor institutions, except to the extent that those laws are inconsistent with any provision of this title, and then only to the extent of the inconsistency. The Board is authorized to determine whether such inconsistencies exist. The Board may not determine that any such law is inconsistent with any provision of this title if the Board determines that such law requires the maintenance of records with greater geographic or other detail than is required under this title, or that such law otherwise provides greater disclosure than is required under this title.

(b) The Board may by regulation exempt from the requirements of this title any State chartered depository institution within any State or subdivision thereof if it determines that, under the law of such State or subdivision, that institution is subject to requirements substantially similar to those imposed under this title, and that such law contains adequate provisions for enforcement. Notwithstanding any other provision of this subsection, compliance with the requirements imposed under this subsection shall be enforced under--

(1) section 8 of the Federal Deposit Insurance Act in the case of national banks, by the Comptroller of the Currency; and

(2) section 8 of the Federal Deposit Insurance Act, by the Director of the Office of Thrift Supervision in the case of a savings association the deposits of which are insured by the Federal Deposit Insurance Corporation.

[Codified to 12 U.S.C. 2805]

[Source: Section 306 of title III of the Act of December 31, 1975 (Pub. L. No. 94--209; 89 Stat. 1127), effective June 28, 1976; as amended by section 1087(b) of the Act of November 7, 1988 (Pub. L. No. 100--628; 102 Stat. 3280), effective November 7, 1988; section 744(p)(2)

of title VII of the Act of August 9, 1989 (Pub. L. No. 101--73; 103 Stat. 440), effective August 9, 1989]

{{4-28-00 p.7308}}

RESEARCH AND IMPROVED METHODS

SEC. 307. (a)(1) The Director of the Office of Thrift Supervision, with the assistance of the Secretary, the Director of the Bureau of the Census, the Comptroller of the Currency, the Board of Governors of the Federal Reserve System, the Federal Deposit Insurance Corporation, and such other persons as the Director of the Office of Thrift Supervision deems appropriate, shall develop or assist in the improvement of, methods of matching addresses and census tracts to facilitate compliance by depository institutions in as economical a manner as possible with the requirements of this title.

(2) There is authorized to be appropriated such sums as may be necessary to carry out this subsection.

(3) The Director of the Office of Thrift Supervision is authorized to utilize, contract with, act through, or compensate any person or agency in order to carry out this subsection.

(b) The Director of the Office of Thrift Supervision shall recommend to the Committee on Banking, Currency and Housing of the House of Representatives and the Committee on Banking, Finance and Urban Affairs of the Senate such additional legislation as the Director of the Office of Thrift Supervision deems appropriate to carry out the purpose of this title.

[Codified to 12 U.S.C. 2806]

[Source: Section 307 of title III of the Act of December 31, 1975 (Pub. L. No. 94--200; 89 Stat. 1127), effective June 28, 1976; as amended by section 1087(c) of the Act of November 7, 1988 (Pub. L. No. 100-

-628; 102 Stat. 3280), effective November 7, 1988; section 744(p)(3) of title VII of the Act of August 9, 1989 (Pub. L. No. 101--73; 103 Stat. 440), effective August 9, 1989]

STUDY

SEC. 308. The Board, in consultation with the Secretary of Housing and Urban Development, shall report annually to the Congress on the utility of the requirements of section 304(b)(4).

[Codified to 12 U.S.C. 2807]

[Source: Section 308 of title III of the Act of December 31, 1975 (Pub. L. No. 94--200; 89 Stat. 1128), effective June 28, 1976; as amended by section 701(b) of title VII of the Act of November 30, 1983 (Pub. L. No. 98--181; 97 Stat. 1266 effective November 30, 1983; section 1211(h) of title XII of the Act of August 9, 1989 (Pub. L. No. 101--73; 103 Stat. 526), effective August 9, 1989]

EFFECTIVE DATE

SEC. 309. (a) In General.--This title shall take effect on the one hundred and eightieth day beginning after the date of its enactment. Any institution specified in section 303(2)(A) which has total assets as of its last full fiscal year of $10,000,000 or less is exempt from the provisions of this title. The Board, in consultation with the Secretary, may exempt institutions described in section 303(2)(B) that are comparable within their respective industries to institutions that are exempt under the preceding sentence (as determined without regard to the adjustment made by subsection (b)).

(b) CPI ADJUSTMENTS.--

(1) IN GENERAL.--Subject to paragraph (2), the dollar amount

applicable with respect to institutions described in section 303(2)(A) under the 2d sentence of subsection (a) shall be adjusted annually after December 31, 1996, by the annual percentage increase in the Consumer Price Index for Urban Wage Earners and Clerical Workers published by the Bureau of Labor Statistics.

(2) 1-TIME ADJUSTMENT FOR PRIOR INFLATION.--The first adjustment made under paragraph (1) after the date of the enactment of the Economic Growth and Regulatory Paperwork Reduction Act of 1996 shall be the percentage by which--

{{4-28-00 p.7309}}

(A) the Consumer Price Index described in such paragraph for the calendar year 1996, exceeds

(B) such Consumer Price Index for the calendar year 1975.

(3) ROUNDING.--The dollar amount applicable under paragraph (1) for any calendar year shall be the amount determined in accordance with subparagraphs (A) and (B) of paragraph (2) and rounded to the nearest multiple of $1,000,00.

[Codified to 12 U.S.C. 2808]

[Source: Section 309 of title III of the Act of December 31, 1975 (Pub. L. No. 94--200; 89 Stat. 1128), effective June 28, 1976; as amended by section 224(a) of title II of the Act of December 19, 1991 (Pub. L. No. 102--242; 105 Stat. 2307), effective January 1, 1992; section 2225(a) of title II of the Act of September 30, 1996 (Pub. L. No. 104-208; 110 Stat. 3009-415), effective September 30, 1996]

COMPILATION OF AGGREGATE DATA

SEC. 310. (a) Beginning with data for calendar year 1980, the Federal Financial Institutions Examination Council shall compile each year, for each primary metropolitan statistical area, metropolitan statistical area, or consolidated metropolitan statistical area that is not comprised of designated primary metropolitan statistical areas, aggregate data by census tract for all depository institutions which are required to disclose data under section 304 or which are exempt pursuant to section 306(b). The Council shall also produce tables indicating, for each primary metropolitan statistical area, metropolitan statistical area, or consolidated metropolitan statistical area that is not comprised of designated primary metropolitan statistical areas, aggregate lending patterns for various categories of census tracts grouped according to location, age of housing stock, income level, and racial characteristics.

(b) The Board shall provide staff and data processing resources to the Council to enable it to carry out the provisions of subsection (a).

(c) The data and tables required pursuant to subsection (a) shall be made available to the public by no later than December 31 of the year following the calendar year on which the data is based.

[Codified to 12 U.S.C. 2809]

[Source: Section 310 of title III of the Act of December 31, 1975 (Pub. L. No. 94--200; 89 Stat. 1128), effective June 28, 1976; as amended by section 340 of title III of the Act of October 8, 1980 (Pub. L. No. 96--399; 94 Stat. 1658), effective October 8, 1980; section 701(a) of title VII of the Act of November 30, 1983 (Pub. L. No. 98--181; 97 Stat. 1266), effective November 30, 1983]

DISCLOSURE BY THE SECRETARY

SEC. 311. Beginning with data for calendar year 1980, the Secretary shall make publicly available data in the Secretary's possession for each mortgagee which is not otherwise subject to the requirements of this title and which is not exempt pursuant to section 306(b) (and for each mortgagee making mortgage loans exempted under section 304(g)), with respect to mortgage loans approved (or for which completed applications are received) by the Secretary for insurance under title I or II of the National Housing Act. Such data to be disclosed shall consist of data comparable to the data which would be disclosed if such mortgagee were subject to the requirements of section 304. Disclosure statements containing data for each such mortgagee for a primary metropolitan statistical area, metropolitan statistical area, or consolidated metropolitan statistical area that is not comprised of designated primary metropolitan statistical areas, shall, at a minimum, be publicly available at the central depository of data established pursuant to section 304(f) for such primary metropolitan statistical area, metropolitan statistical area, or consolidated metropolitan statistical area that is not comprised of designated primary metropolitan statistical areas. The Secretary shall also compile and make publicly available aggregate {{4-28-00 p.7310}}data for such mortgagees by census tract, and tables indicating aggregate lending patterns, in a manner comparable to the information required to be made publicly available in accordance with section 310.

[Codified to 12 U.S.C. 2810]

[Source: Section 340 of title III of the Act of October 8, 1980 (Pub. L. No. 96--399; 94 Stat. 1658), effective October 8, 1980; as amended by section 701(a) of title VII of the Act of November 30, 1983 (Pub. L. No. 98--181; 97 Stat. 1266), effective November 30, 1983; section 565(a)(3) of title V of the Act of February 5, 1988 (Pub. L. No. 100--242; 101 Stat 1945), effective February 5, 1988; and section 1211(c)(D) of title XII of the Act of August 9, 1989 (Pub. L. No. 101--73; 103 Stat. 525), effective August 9, 1989]

The information above was found on www.fdic.gov.

APPENDIX 5

Home Mortgage Disclosure Act Regulation C
(from www.ffiec.gov/hmda/history.htm)

BACKGROUND & PURPOSE

The Home Mortgage Disclosure Act (HMDA) was enacted by Congress in 1975 and is implemented by the Federal Reserve Board's Regulation C. This regulation provides the public loan data that can be used to assist:

§   in determining whether financial institutions are serving the housing needs of their communities;

§   public officials in distributing public-sector investments so as to attract private investment to areas where it is needed;

§   and in identifying possible discriminatory lending patterns.

This regulation applies to certain financial institutions, including banks, savings associations, credit unions, and other mortgage lending institutions. In 2005, there were approximately 33.6 million loan records for calendar year (CY) 2004 reported by 8,853 financial institutions. In 2004, 8,121 financial institutions reported approximately 41.6 million loan records for CY 2003. In 2003, 7,771 financial institutions reported approximately 31 million loan records for CY 2002. In 2002, 7,631 financial institutions reported approximately 28 million loan records for CY 2001. In 2001, 7,713 financial institutions reported approximately 19 million loan records for CY 2000. In 2000, 7,829 financial institutions reported approximately 23 million loan records for CY 1999. In 1999, 7,836 financial institutions reported approximately 24.7 million loan records for CY 1998. In 1998, 7,925 financial institutions reported approximately 16.4 million loan records for CY 1997.

Using the loan data submitted by these financial institutions, the Federal Financial Institutions Examination Council (FFIEC) creates aggregate and disclosure reports for each metropolitan area (MA) that are available to the public at central data depositories located in each MA. The MA aggregate and disclosure reports for calendar years 1997 - 2003 are available on this web site. Furthermore, the FFIEC provides to the public various electronic, paper and magnetic media items available through the FFIEC's web sites and data request order form.

APPENDIX 6

Equal Credit Opportunity Act

Regulation B

Regulation B was issued by the Board of Governors of the Federal Reserve System to implement the provisions of the Equal Credit Opportunity Act (ECOA). The law was enacted in 1974 to make it unlawful for creditors to discriminate in any aspect of a credit transaction on the basis of sex or marital status. In 1976, through amendments to the Act, it became unlawful to also discriminate on the basis of race, color, religion, national origin, age, receipt of public assistance and the good faith exercise of rights under the Consumer Credit Protection Act.

The primary purpose of the ECOA is to prevent discrimination in the granting of credit by requiring banks and other creditors to make extensions of credit equally available to all creditworthy applicants with fairness, impartiality and without discrimination on any prohibited basis. The regulation applies to consumer and other types of credit transactions. This discussion will be limited to those provisions of ECOA that relate specifically to the mortgage lending process, including:

1. **Rules Concerning Taking of Applications**

2. **Rules Concerning the Evaluation of Applications**

3. Rules Concerning Extension of Credit

4. Consumer Notifications

5. Consumer Information for Monitoring Purposes

Rules Concerning Taking of Applications

Oral or Written Statements:

The regulation specifically prohibits a lender from making any oral or written statement, in advertising or otherwise, to applicants or prospective applicants that would discourage on a prohibited basis a responsible person from making or pursuing an application.

Collection of Information:

With regards to collection of information, a lender may request any information in connection with an application, with certain exceptions discussed below:

- **Required collection of information:** The lender is required to request information for monitoring purposes for credit transactions secured by the applicant's dwelling.

- **Information about a spouse or former spouse:** The lender is permitted under the regulation to request any information concerning an applicant's spouse that is requested about the applicant, if the applicant resides in a community property state, like California, or property on which the applicant is relying as a basis for repayment of the credit requested is located in a community property state. Information regarding a former spouse may be requested if the request can also be made to the applicant, if the applicant is relying upon alimony, child support or separate maintenance payments from a spouse (no longer residing with the applicant) or former spouse as a basis for repayment of the credit requested.

- **Other accounts of the applicant:** A lender may request an applicant to list any account upon which the applicant is liable and to provide the name and address in which the account is carried. A lender may also ask the names in which an applicant has previously received credit.

- **Marital status:** In California, a lender may inquire about an applicant's marital status, due to the fact that California is a community property state. A lender may only use the terms "married", "unmarried" and "separated".

- **Disclosure about income from alimony, child support or separate maintenance:** Under the regulation, a lender may inquire whether an applicant's income is derived in whole or part from alimony, child support or separate maintenance only if the lender first discloses to the applicant that the income from these sources need not be revealed unless the applicant wishes to rely on it to establish creditworthiness. This disclosure must be given to any co-applicant as well.

- **Sex:** Lender is prohibited from inquiring about the sex of an applicant. An applicant may be requested to designate a title in an application form (such as Ms., Mr., Mrs. or Miss) if the form discloses that the title designation is optional. Otherwise, the application form must use terms that are neutral to sex.

- **Childbearing, childrearing:** The lender is prohibited from requesting or considering information concerning the applicant's plan or expectations of having children, their childbearing capabilities or birth-control practices. The lender is permitted to inquire about the number and ages of an applicant's dependents or about dependent-related financial obligations or expenditures, provided such information is requested without regard to any prohibited basis.

- **Race, color, religion, national origin:** A lender may not inquire about the race, color, religion or national origin of any applicant or any other person in connection with a credit transaction. A lender may inquire about an applicant's permanent residence and immigration status.

Rules Concerning Evaluation of Applications

Evaluation of Information:

The regulation allows a lender to consider any information properly obtained, so long as the information is not used to discriminate against an applicant on a prohibited basis.

Specific Rules Concerning the Use of Information:

- A lender may not take a prohibited basis into account in any system of evaluating the creditworthiness of applicants.

- Age and/or receipt of public assistance may only be used for the purpose of determining a pertinent element of creditworthiness. Furthermore, age may be considered when such age is used to favor the elderly applicant in extending credit.

- Childbearing, childrearing assumptions or aggregate statistics relating to the likelihood that any group of persons will bear or rear children or will, for that reason, receive diminished or interrupted income in the future, may not be used by the lender.

- A lender may not take into account whether there is a telephone listing in the name of the applicant for the consumer credit, but may take into account whether there is a telephone in the applicant's residence.

- A lender may not discount or exclude from consideration the income of an applicant or the spouse of an applicant on a prohibited basis or because the income is derived from part-time employment or is an annuity, pension or other retirement benefit. A lender may consider that amount and the probable continuance of any such income in evaluating an applicant's creditworthiness.

- To the extent that a lender considers credit history in evaluating the creditworthiness of similarly qualified applicants for a similar type and amount of credit in evaluating an applicant's creditworthiness, a lender may consider:

- The credit history, when available, of accounts designated as accounts that the applicant and that applicant's spouse are permitted to use or for which both are contractually liable;

- On the applicant's request, any information the applicant may present that tends to indicate that the credit does not accurately reflect the applicant's creditworthiness; and

- On the applicant's request, the credit history, when available, of any account reported in the name of the applicant's spouse or former spouse that the applicant can demonstrate accurately reflects the applicant's creditworthiness.

Rules Concerning Extension of Credit

Extension of Credit:

A lender may not refuse to grant an individual account to a creditworthy applicant on the basis of sex, marital status or any other prohibited basis.

Applicant's Name(s):

A lender may not refuse to allow an applicant to open or maintain an account in a birth-given first name and surname that is the applicant's birth-given surname, the spouse's surname or a combined surname.

Signature of Applicant's Spouse or Other Person:

In general, a lender may not require the signature of an applicant's spouse or other person, other than a joint applicant, on any credit instrument if the applicant qualifies under the lender's standards of creditworthiness for the amount and terms of the credit requested. If an individual applicant requests credit to be secured, the lender may require the signature of the applicant's spouse or other joint owner of the collateral on any instrument necessary or reasonably believed to be necessary under state law to make the property being offered as security available to satisfy the debt in the event of a default. In California, applicable state law requires all owners of personal property to sign in order to encumber the property. Therefore, the lender may request the non-applicant spouse or other parties to sign a security agreement or other instrument to secure a lien on the property, but not the promissory note. With transactions involving community real property, both spouses must sign the deed of trust in order for the lien to be perfected for the lender. Non-applicant spouse's signature should never be requested on the application or the promissory note.

Consumer Notifications:

Appraisal Notification:

Effective December 14, 1993, the Federal Reserve Board issued amendments to Regulation B, Equal Credit Opportunity Act. These amendments require the lender to notify the applicant of their right to receive a copy of their appraisal on loans secured by one-to-four family dwellings.

Action Taken:

A lender must notify an applicant of action taken generally within 30 days after receiving a completed application. A notification given to an applicant when adverse action is taken is required to be in writing and must contain: a statement of action taken; the name and address of the lender; a statement of the provisions known commonly as the ECOA Notice; the name and address of the federal agency that administers compliance with respect to the lender; and either a statement of specific reasons for the action taken or a disclosure of the applicant's right to a statement of specific reasons within 30 a specified period of time.

Information for Monitoring Purposes:

A lender that receives an application for credit primarily for the purchase or refinancing of a dwelling occupied or to be occupied by the applicant as a principal residence, where the extension of credit will be secured by the dwelling, is required to request as part of the application the following information regarding the applicant: race or national origin (using the categories American Indian or Alaskan Native; Asian or Pacific Islander; Black; White; Hispanic; Other (specify)); sex; marital Status (using the categories Married, Unmarried, and Separated); and age.

The applicant(s) are not required to supply the requested information. If the applicant(s) chooses not to provide the requested information or any part of it, that fact will be noted on the form. The lender then is required to note on the form, to the extent possible, the race and national origin and sex of the applicant(s) on the basis of visual observation or surname.

The lender is required to inform the applicant(s) that the governmental information is being requested by the federal government for the purpose of monitoring compliance with the federal statutes that prohibit lender from discriminating against applicants on the basis of race or national origin, sex, martial status and age. The lender should also inform the applicant(s) that if the applicant chooses not to provide the information, the lender is required to note the race or national origin and sex on the basis of visual observation.

If you are thinking about purchasing or refinancing a home, feel free to check out the CD included in the back of this book. It contains an application that allows you to securely connect with "Origination Fee Free" loans from our affiliates who have agreed to waive all origination fees. There is no cost to use the application, and no obligation to use any of the offered loans.